Praise for the breakthrough solutions in
400 Ways to Stop Stress Now...and Forever!

From experts:

"We live our lives oftentimes mired in destructive habits of insecurity—habits that generate anxiety and stress. G. Gaynor McTigue has managed to compile a profound and unique array of eye-opening life strategies that offer the reader simple, effective and healthy alternatives to stress. If stress is part of your life, you can't afford not to read this wonderful book."
> —Dr. Joe Luciani, author of *Self-Coaching: The Powerful Program to Beat Anxiety and Depression*

* * *

"Open this book anywhere and you will enjoy common sense solutions to life's big and small problems. It is like having a wise advisor at your fingertips."
> —Gloria Arenson, MS, MFT, author of *Five Simple Steps to Emotional Healing*

* * *

"If you're looking for a variety of quick and effective ideas for lowering your stress level, you can hardly do better than G. Gaynor McTigue's new book. There is literally a lot of something for everyone!"
> —Jeff Davidson, author the *60 Second Organizer*

* * *

"Did my family bribe McTigue to write this book? It's the reliable advice from those who know exactly what I need to do to be happy. And they...and McTigue...are absolutely right. And it's all dished out in digestible bite sized tidbits!"
> —Carolyn Reuben, author of *Cleansing the Body, Mind, and Spirit*

From readers around the world:

"Stress tips? Fantastic! More like practical wisdom for living. They have helped to streamline life, refocus on priorities, endorse my humanity, appreciate diversity, accept my limitations, welcome beauty, question status quo, challenge norms, and regain composure when the frenzy of busyness escalates!"
    —Marisa, London, UK

* * *

"Like a sharp, merciless scalpel, these stress tips cut away the fluff, the fads, the senseless distractions in our culture that tend to rob us of who we are."
    —Linda Maxwell, Richmond, KY

* * *

"Commom sense, easily identifiable situations and behaviours that leave me laughing at myself because they are *us!* Thank you for your insights and helping me to leave behind the rat race. I thought I was alone in my dissatisfaction of our way of life until I read your many eloquent words."
    —Bernadette Keane, USA

* * *

"Brilliantly simple, easy to put into practice and particularly relevant to our modern lifestyle!"
    —Jeanette, Queensland, Australia

* * *

"G. Gaynor McTigue writes in a clear, straightforward, practical way that will soon help clear the mental and physical clutter from your life, eradicate the thinking errors and set you on a course for a happier, healthier existence."
    —Jeff Petersen, Cove, Oregon

400
Ways to
Stop *Stress* Now...
and Forever!

G. Gaynor McTigue

G. Gaynor McTigue

Pick Me **Up** Books

400 Ways to Stop *Stress* Now...and Forever!

A Solution for Virtually Every Stressful Situation You Face

For information about special discounts for bulk purchases, please contact Pick Me Up Books at 203-254-7789. Or email: pickmeupbooks@aol.com

This book is not intended to take the
place of professional therapy.

ISBN 978-0-9716427-1-3

Library of Congress Control Number: 2006930384

Printed in the United States of America

www.pickmeupbooks.com

To Owen and Katherine

Fast-Find Stress Relief Guide

Use this index to get immediate solutions for the stress, anxiety and clutter you may be experiencing right now.

Work Stress

Rushing-Around Stress

Rushing-Around Stress (cont'd)

Parenting Stress

Relationship Stress

Relationship Stress (cont'd)

Mental Stress

Mental Stress (cont'd)

Health-Related Stress

Household Stress

Communication Stress (cont'd)

Recreational Stress Relievers

Reversing Stressful Habits & Mindsets (cont'd)

Reversing Stressful Habits & Mindsets (cont'd)

Reversing Stressful Habits & Mindsets (cont'd)

Introduction

Several years ago I wrote a book called *Life's Little Frustration Book* (St. Martin's Press). It was a humor book, a collection of all those irritating and annoying things that happen to us. For example: *You can't open a drawer because something inside it is sticking up, and you can't push it down until you open the drawer.*

And in doing that book, I realized what a complicated mess our lives have become, how little room we leave for error, how tightly our days are packed, so if only one thing doesn't go as planned...everything starts to unravel. So we often find ourselves rushed, frustrated, frazzled...*stressed out.* Living almost our entire lives in crisis mode. And we weren't made for that. Sure, we can handle a pressure situation once in a while. But all the time? Think of the wear and tear on your nerves. All those harmful hormones and free radicals you're unleashing—day after day, year after year—weakening your immune system, contributing to illnesses, aging you prematurely. Surely there must be something out there that can help put a stop to this madness.

And it occurred to me that if all the countless available stress "remedies"—books, videos, drugs, audio tapes, aroma therapy, vibrating chairs, relaxation techniques, programs, devices—are so effective, *how come everyone is still stressed out?*

The answer is simple. While these methods may help to *ease* your stress—that is, treat its symptoms—most of them do little or nothing to *eliminate the causes*, to *reverse* the stressful habits, attitudes and mind-sets you've developed over the course of your life.

And that's the primary mission of this book. The solutions contained herein will give you the tools, motivation and attitude changes you need to root out stress at its very source...on the multiple battlefronts of your life: work, home, travel, parenting, relationships, food, finances, shopping, entertaining, school, and many other areas. You'll find a specific strategy for virtually every stressful situation you face.

The tone of the book is frank and direct—at times even scolding. The intention is to mimic your own inner voice, exhorting you to slow it down, do it right, stop making everything more complicated than it is. The mere act of reading the book can be liberating in itself. But that will be short-lived unless you commit yourself to making each applicable strategy a permanent part of your life. And that requires frequent re-reading, reeducating and reminding yourself—until the long-term benefits of a calmer, happier existence take hold. The brevity and numbering of the tips make this easy to do. (So you really have no excuse.)

It's time to stop the insanity and take back control of your life. Starting today. Starting *now*. If you're experiencing undue stress at this very moment, you'll want to use the *Fast-Find Stress Relief Guide*. It will help you zero right in on the particular area of your life that's causing the most anxiety and concern.

These strategies are the same ones I teach in the stress workshops I conduct for groups and organizations. In fact, thousands of people worldwide are using them successfully every day. I'm confident they'll work for you, too.

If they do, please recommend this book to others who are overly stressed. The fewer people there are to swim upstream against, the easier our own efforts will be. And perhaps someday, through our example, we can even turn the tide.

G. Gaynor McTigue

1
Do one thing at a time.

Do it mindfully. Do it well. Enjoy the satisfaction. Then go on to the next thing. Multitasking might work for computers, but humans have yet to get the hang of it. A growing body of evidence affirms that trying to accomplish several things at once takes up more time overall than doing them sequentially. It consumes an excessive amount of mental energy, too, so you fatigue more quickly. The lack of focus also leads to careless mistakes, shoddy work and unreliable performance. Worst of all, having to do things over. *This is no way to live.* Give what you're doing your undivided attention. Take the time to get it right. You'll be more productive, and less stressed, in the long run. Why make yourself crazy?

2
Throw something out every day.

You've got too much stuff in your house. Office. Garage. Attic. Useless clutter that's weighing you down, getting in the way, obscuring the things you really need. Just *looking* at the stuff is stressful, to the point where physical clutter soon becomes mental clutter. The problem is getting rid of it. It's a huge job, so you keep putting it off. But the more you put it off the more clutter you accumulate...making it an even more humongous task to face. Here's how to break the cycle. Every day, find one thing you don't need and toss it. Or give it away. Or sell it at a consignment shop. Be realistic. If you're not going to use it, lose it. Over time, the clutter will begin to vanish and space and order will magically appear in your home... and your life. Stick with this. It really works. Why make yourself crazy?

3
Steer clear of negative people.

You know them well: the whiners, the ones who find fault with everything, who always lay a hard luck story on you, who constantly give you grief over harmless trifles, or make wholesale denunciations of people, institutions and cultures that don't suit their fancy or conform to their way of thinking. Unless you're stuck with them, shun them. They'll pull you down, darken your outlook, try to make your life as miserable as theirs. Who needs that? And if you *are* stuck with them (relatives, coworkers, housemates) don't agree with or encourage them. In fact, say nothing and simply leave the scene whenever they launch into one of their diatribes. Why make yourself crazy?

4
Have small, intimate get-togethers.

Big parties are expensive, time-consuming and a heck of a lot of work. Even if you're lucky enough to talk with everyone, it may only amount to brief, cursory snippets of conversation. A big bash can be fun, sure, if you're not the one throwing it. Smaller parties are easier to arrange, less work, less expensive, and leave lots of time to enjoy your guests, who feel more special, too. Entertain fewer people...more often. Why make yourself crazy?

5
Work changes into your life gradually.

No crash diets. No sudden, intense workout programs. No radical overhauls of who and what you are. You might maintain it for a while, but it can't last. True change takes lots of small, mindful, subtle decisions over time that add up to bigger, more enduring transformations. They're less disruptive to you and everyone else, and inevitably get the results you want. Be patient. If you're really intent on change, you should develop the staying power to achieve it without having to act rashly. Do it by degrees. Why make yourself crazy?

6
Cut down on competitive stress.

Today, we compete for everything: the space around us, to be first to own a new product, to get our kids signed up for programs, to get our viewpoints across, to be faster, smarter, richer, sexier. Our days are filled with stressful competitions. And most are absolutely unnecessary. Because they're driven by insecurity, fear of being left behind, an ingrained need to always have more or better than the next guy. Try to get above all that. If you want to compete, vie to be the one who stays calm and in control, who isn't easily sucked in by material things, who avoids being caught up in the daily grab-bag that robs people of health and peace of mind. Compete for that and see how pointless all those other competitions become. And how misguided those who partake in them begin to appear. Why make yourself crazy?

7
It's not what happens to you, it's how you react.

In any given day, you'll have progress and set-backs, triumphs and failures. That you can bet on. But as good a day as some people have, they'll manage to find something to fret about. ("It's just luck, it won't last, I'm destined for misery.") And as bad a day as others have, they'll see the good in it. ("So what? I'm still alive, still kicking and nothing's going to stop me.") Which attitude will win over your day? And the next day? And the next? You have control over that: to enjoy your accomplishments without diminishing them; to accept your failures as opportunities to learn. You have the power to make every day a positive outcome. Because it's not what happens to you, it's how you react to it. Why make yourself crazy?

8
One sport per child per season.

There are more than enough opportunities during the year for your child to participate in different sports, without having to cram several into one season. Shuttling kids around like a madman on weekends stresses out the entire family, at a time when everyone should be stress-*free*. It also isn't fair to coaches and teammates when conflicts cause your child to miss important games and practices. Why over-plan leisure? Kids should have ample free time for unstructured play to let their imaginations take flight, rather than always be saddled with adult-like schedules. Limit each child to a single sport per season. He or she can focus on it, get better at it, and you can enjoy watching it. You'll also have more time together as a family. Why make yourself crazy?

9
Don't flip out choosing wallpaper.

Or a paint color. A tie. Fabric. Even an ice cream flavor. There are enough choices out there to freak us all out. So try this. Make the selection process a series of one-on-one competitions. Pick a style or variety that's appealing, then try to beat it. If you succeed, discard the first and try to knock off the second. And so on. It's a lot less mystifying than attempting to evaluate a whole bunch of selections at once. When you finally find something you can't beat...*buy*. Why make yourself crazy?

10
Don't overload your travel itinerary.

It's one of the biggest mistakes of recreational travel: trying to squeeze in too many cities, sites, museums, tours, side trips, events, and performances, leaving you overwhelmed, exhausted and unable to appreciate much of anything. On your vacation! Better to limit your attractions to what you can leisurely and fully enjoy. With plenty of in-between time to linger over a meal, observe the locals and discover things on your own...the best part of traveling anyway. Don't pressure yourself into seeing everything just to say you have. Why make yourself crazy?

11
Encourage work-related stress management.

If you employ or manage people, you may think that their constantly working under stress means you're getting the most out of them...and getting your money's worth. But, oh, how shortsighted that can be! Chronic work-related stress leads to absenteeism, illness, higher health insurance premiums, job dissatisfaction, mistakes, accidents, tense relationships, and high turnover. Meaning, it's costing you big time! People work better, longer, happier, and more productively when allowed to work in a less stressful environment. Is it any wonder that some of the most successful companies are those that offer stress reduction programs, exercise classes, workout facilities, company outings, and other morale-boosting perks? Get smart. Promote a stress-free workplace. It's good business policy. Why make yourself crazy?

12
Avoid eating as a response to stress.

Remember when people used to grab a cigarette during moments of stress? Thankfully, most have managed to kick the habit. Now unfortunately it's food many of us reach for at such times, for both good stress and bad. Be careful. Monitor yourself in these situations. Do you want that snack because you're genuinely hungry? Or are you just looking for a way to dissipate some anxiety? Adding excess calories and unwanted weight will only lock you into a harmful stress/eating cycle. Try other instant stress relievers like the many others you'll find in this book: slow deep breathing, standing up and stretching, taking walks, meditating. Curb the urge to eat your way out of tight situations. Why make yourself crazy?

13
Be the director of your own life.

In Hollywood—or anywhere else for that matter— everyone wants to direct. And well they should. Maybe not a motion picture. But something more important. Their lives. When you see yourself as producer, writer and director of your own life, enormous possibilities open up...untold power is yours. You choose the setting. You choose the role you want to play. You fashion the dialogue. You direct the action. If you think the script you now live by is tired and worn, or too fast-paced, simply rewrite it. As its author, use your imagination to achieve a spirited mix of adventure, comedy and drama. Then, grabbing the leading role, go out and live it. Why make yourself crazy?

14
Eliminate meaningless deadlines.

Our lives have become one long game of beat the clock. Crammed with arbitrary and unrealistic time constraints imposed by ourselves and others that serve only to make us more pressured, anxious and stressed out. *For no worthwhile reason.* Avoid the trap of assigning timeframes to everything you do, especially if you have little idea how long it will take. But, you say, I *need* a deadline or I simply won't get around to doing it. If that's the case, it's not a deadline you need, it's a goal. Make your goal one of completing a project in a careful, professional, satisfying manner. In other words, as long as it takes to do it right. Or maybe your goal is to make the project more fun and interesting, or to develop a new and more expedient way of doing it. In any case, save your nerves and your energy for the few *real* deadlines we face...like April 15th. Why make yourself crazy?

15
Don't equate saving with buying things on sale.

Real saving takes sacrifice. Doing without. And putting money away. But we've been deceived, or are deceiving ourselves, into thinking we're saving money by spending it. That's why everything is almost always on sale. (Which makes you suspect it's overpriced to begin with.) So when they tell you to act now or lose out on big savings, don't buy it. Wait until you really need the item. Chances are you'll find it on sale anyway. Why keep chasing after so-called "savings" that just put you further into debt? Why make yourself crazy?

16
Don't feed a foul mood.

You're angry, disgusted, fed up, deflated, or demoralized. That's when it's easiest to gang up on yourself, to paint every little thing that happens to you the color of your dark outlook. Perversely building a case for your impending downfall. Nonsense. You're merely prolonging the time it takes to tough it through a difficult state of mind. Kick the "woe is me" syndrome as quickly as possible. Rather than brood, get distracted by other activities and pursuits. Engage yourself in work, exercise or social interaction. In short order, your mood will lift like a gloomy fog swept away in a stiff breeze. Why make yourself crazy?

17
Have backups of essential items in place.

So that you never run out of critical oft-used household staples like laundry detergent, milk, deodorant, toothpaste, batteries, or bathroom tissue... employ the buy-two-replace-one method. For example, buy two bottles of mouthwash. That way you'll have an immediate replacement when the first one is used up, which will give you ample time to buy another before you run out of the second. Make a list of those items it would be more than a little stressful to have to go without—there really shouldn't be many— and see to it you've got both the item and its backup on hand. Why make yourself crazy?

18
Don't get hung up on product features.

The more bells and whistles a product has, the more there is to learn and remember, the more complicated it is to use and the more expensive it is to buy. Save yourself the waste and aggravation of over-buying your need. Get a unit that serves your main purpose simply and economically, with maybe one or two extras you'll definitely use. Loading up on the latest gimmickry will cost you in more ways than one. There's nothing more annoying than having to reread instructions every time you use something. Why make yourself crazy?

19
Don't carry the world upon your shoulders.

So the song goes. And how true. There's enough crime, starvation, wretchedness, injustice, depravity and evil out there to drag us into utter despair every day...if we choose to let it. Do yourself a favor. Don't. Recognize that there's little most of us can do as individuals to make wholesale changes in the world. But within the sphere of our own lives, there's plenty we can do. Try kindness, generosity, understanding, and love. Starting with your own family and working your way out. And guess what? When you add up these individual contributions from all of us, it *can* make a difference in the world. So take care of the local stuff and the rest will follow. Why make yourself crazy?

20
Leave a cushion of time
between events.

Scheduling appointments, meetings, projects, luncheons, and events too closely together is a guaranteed stress fest. It leaves you vulnerable to even the slightest delays, which *will* occur. You'll always have one eye on the clock and thus be distracted, rushed and prone to miss things and make mistakes. Be smart. Don't stack up your events like planes on a runway. Life never works out that efficiently. Spread your schedule out. Always leave sufficient in-between time to allow for any unexpected bumps and delays. It will not go to waste. You'll be glad to have those breaks to answer phone calls and email messages, take care of incidental things, and prepare yourself for your next event. That extra cushion of time will leave you less frazzled, and more productive, in the long run. Why make yourself crazy?

21
Develop a gift ear.

Constantly coming up with fresh and innovative gifts for birthdays, anniversaries and holidays can be an exasperating challenge. A carefully selected gift certificate from the recipient's favorite store or service is one way to go. Here's another. Always keep a sharp ear open. In the course of casual conversation, people unwittingly reveal needs and yearnings that can trigger incredibly on-target gift ideas. You just have to train yourself to "hear" them. When you do, write them down immediately since it's likely you'll forget. Don't be a perpetually stumped gift giver. Turn on your gift radar starting today. Why make yourself crazy?

22
Always view yourself as ahead, not behind.

This small change in perspective can alter your approach to everything. When you perpetually see yourself behind schedule, never caught up, forever lacking in something...your emphasis is always on need. And that puts unrelenting, unhealthy pressure on you. But view yourself as ahead of the game (and most of us truly are) and the pressure almost immediately eases, and your needs diminish, because you're grateful for what you already have. You can move forward confidently from a position of strength, rather than struggle from one of weakness. It's all in the way you look at it. Why make yourself crazy?

23
Don't over-volunteer.

Resist volunteering for more than you can handle, more than your free time allows. Volunteering is great, but heavy involvement can steal important time from your family and relationships. (And it shouldn't be used as an excuse to avoid more important obligations.) If the work becomes too demanding, simply say no. Nobody else is going to look out for you better than yourself. If we all "volunteered" to spend more time with the kids, visit our parents, make loving homes, and carve out special time for ourselves, there wouldn't be a need for so much volunteering in the first place. Why make yourself crazy?

24
Entrust responsibility to responsible people.

There are those who always have a convenient excuse for not getting it right, showing up late or botching the job entirely. And there are those who consistently, effectively and unequivocally come through for you. This isn't luck. It's responsibility. Not something you're born with. Something you do. Responsibility takes effort. Concern. Pride. And perseverance. Whom do you want to entrust your children, your home, your finances, and your other important responsibilities to? Lose the whiners and stick with the winners. Why make yourself crazy?

25
Know when to go with a pro.

It's very satisfying when you can complete a project yourself, without having to resort to professional help. And that's great. But there are some projects—either because they're too complex, dangerous, extremely messy, or require several people—you should simply stay away from. Know what they are. Before you take on a task that may be out of your league, talk to others who have undertaken a similar project and learn from their experience and mistakes. Or read up about it. It could save you untold time, trouble and misspent energy. Why make yourself crazy?

26
Don't say it, do it.

Boasting about the wonderful things you're *going* to do for yourself and others can actually be your *undoing*. For one, now you're expected to do them. Secondly, if you don't do them you appear weak, unreliable and irresponsible. If you really want to impress people, don't reveal what you intend to do...but simply do it. They'll be surprised and pleased with your accomplishment, and even more moved by your modesty. And if for some reason you can't get it done, no one will be the wiser. Why make yourself crazy?

27
If your kids can't play together nicely, separate them.

How many times do you need to go in and scold your kids for fighting and squabbling? Only once, if you play it smart. When they can't get along, separate them. Deny them the privilege of each other's company until they can work out a peaceful solution. It teaches them the valuable skills of compromise and negotiation. It will make them appreciate each other more. And will give you a needed break. So when the kids start going at it, divide and conquer. Why make yourself crazy?

28
Read ingredient and nutrition labels.

Just because it's a brand name, comes in glitzy packaging and people gush over it in commercials doesn't make it wholesome or nutritious. Thankfully, laws require companies to come clean and list ingredients and nutrition information on their products. Don't ignore it. It's far more revealing than their advertising. Find out how much sugar they're laying on you and your family. (The amounts contained in many foods and beverages will floor you.) Note the number of calories—and grams of protein, fat and carbohydrates—you're consuming. And if you have to be a chemistry major to understand a label, maybe you should pass on it altogether. Get serious about what you're putting into your body. Why make yourself crazy?

29
Accept that people think differently than you do.

You could spend your entire life trying to win over people to your point of view. The simple truth is, you won't. At least, not everyone. Even if you present the most logical, rational, airtight arguments, some people will never see it your way. Maybe they're proud, stubborn, stupid, or in some instances—did you ever stop to think?—*right*. Don't waste your time trying to convert the diehards. Instead, work with them, live with them, respect their differences, and be thankful the world isn't full of people exactly like you. Why make yourself crazy?

30
Adjust your clothes to the ambient temperature.

Why keep your overcoat on in a stifling department store? Or spend time in the chill outdoor air without a jacket? Putting on or peeling off as needed will help you stay comfortable, perform better and enjoy the activity you're involved in. Wear layers that allow you to adjust to the environment. Take advantage of coat checks and lockers. Bring along an extra garment just in case (like tying a sweater around your waist). And don't let what others are wearing, or not wearing, pressure you into the wrong attire. Dress intelligently. Live comfortably. Why make yourself crazy?

31
Don't be a slave to your image.

How much unnecessary stress, excessive work and lost time with loved ones do you incur in the name of how you look to others? Are where you live, what you drive, how you dress, whom you socialize with, and where you send your kids to school dictated more by what's best for you and your family...or by the image you want to project? Carefully scrutinize your motives. You may find that a simpler lifestyle within your means might leave you with less of what impresses others...but more of what makes your life easier, happier and more fulfilling. Why make yourself crazy?

32
Keep your dinner guests out of the kitchen.

What could be more nerve-wracking than trying to prepare a meal while your guests are pelting you with questions, getting in your way, engaging you in distracting conversation? To avoid this, strive to have things pretty much wrapped up by the time people arrive. Barring that, if they do attempt to infiltrate your cooking space, lure them out with a dish of irresistible hors d'oeuvres and join them briefly in another room. Then subtly excuse yourself and slip away to finish preparations. Why make yourself crazy?

33
Keep like things in like places.

Don't store the tennis rackets in the closet and the balls in the garage. Or the vacuum cleaner in the basement and the bags in the attic. It's hard enough to remember where one thing is kept much less two or even three related items. And it's more work fetching them. Store like things together so you'll know exactly where they'll be. Why make yourself crazy?

34
Take the back roads.

Yes, it will take more time, but the trip will be fun, relaxing and enjoyable...and thus go faster. Back roads offer one-of-a-kind sights, interesting people and unique local ambience, while high-speed super-highways drone on with the blandest scenery and tedious driving. Not to mention those cloned service areas. Make getting there a learning, enriching experience. Stop often. Explore. And arrive safe and refreshed. Why make yourself crazy?

35
Find a diverting pastime.

Don't have a hobby of your own? An oasis of joyful distraction? A getaway pursuit that totally absorbs you and counterbalances your hectic existence? Then it's high time you found one. Think of something you'd really enjoy doing. *Really* enjoy doing. Within the confines of respectability, of course. Demand of yourself the free time to pursue it. Once exposed to the pleasures of revitalizing leisure, you won't want to shortchange yourself again. Everyone deserves to have fun once in a while, including you. Why make yourself crazy?

36
Accept that life can be awkward at times.

No matter how carefully you plan things, or imagine they'll turn out, or believe they're supposed to be...some events will leave you confused, uneasy or out of kilter. And you can't explain why. Maybe it's your mood, the alignment of the planets, the weather, your physical condition...or a combination of things. In any case, accept these messy, awkward occasions as part of life. And have faith that things will soon fall back into sync. And you know they will. Why make yourself crazy?

37
Always be equipped for an emergency.

You only need to do this once. In your car, keep a first-aid kit, jumper cables, flares, flashlight, blankets, and a fire extinguisher. Home: a first-aid kit, fire extinguishers, flashlights, candles, and a portable radio. Sports bag: first-aid kit and instant cold packs. Take the time. Make the investment. Do it today. Even if you never use them, the peace of mind alone is worth the effort and expense. Why make yourself crazy?

38
Don't let routine tasks become urgent ones.

Meaning: don't wait until you're out of under-wear before you do your laundry...the fridge is empty before you go shopping...the cell phone dies before you recharge it. That routine task will quickly become a critical one at a time when you can least afford to deal with it. And saddle you with exasperating stress where none should exist. Keep tabs on what might soon need attention and take care of it before it rears up and bites you. Why make yourself crazy?

39
Don't look at your crazed schedule in its entirety.

It'll freak you out...like looking over the edge of a steep cliff. You'll swear you'll never live though it. And stress yourself big time fretting over it. Calm down. Focus only on what you need to accomplish over the next day or so. Deal with each event as it comes. You'll find that things have a way of sorting them-selves out, refreshing breaks do sometimes open up, and other options will present themselves. Your kitchen calendar (or electronic scheduler) can look far more frightening than it really is. One thing at a time. Why make yourself crazy?

40
Don't eat it if you don't want it.

The restaurant serves oversized portions. You take more food than you can eat. You don't want to disappoint your host. You don't like leaving leftovers. You feel guilty throwing food away. Whatever the reason, you often end up eating far more food than you want...or need. This stresses your system, adds unwanted calories and leaves you bloated and full. Don't always feel you have to finish it. In fact, leave the table a little hungry. Overeating can lead to many problems. Why make yourself crazy?

41
Give things a chance.

Today, everyone expects immediate results. So there's a tendency to give up on things too soon—the book you're reading (hopefully not this one!), the mutual fund you've invested in, the musical instrument you're learning, the course you're taking, the person you're dating. Don't be so quick to abandon something that doesn't give you immediate results. This could prevent you from experiencing the greater benefits you'd enjoy by sticking it out longer. Be patient. Give it more time. Find out for certain if something is worthwhile rather than make a hasty departure. It's better than someday regretting you never really gave it a chance. Why make yourself crazy?

42
Turn off the music once in a while.

You don't always have to have the radio going in the house and car. The constant drone of music, talk and noise can grow monotonous, be distracting, interrupt your thought process, become a stressful irritant you're not even aware of. Take a break now and then. Click off the radio and see how naturally relaxing, soothing and refreshing a little quiet can be. And how peaceful it is to hear yourself think. Why make yourself crazy?

43
Draw on your bank of memories.

No one suggests you live in the past. But if the present is so overwhelmingly negative and fraught with problems, you need to neutralize the bad vibes. An effective way to do this is to draw on some of your fondest memories—events, journeys, people, and places that conjure up warm, positive feelings. They'll remind you how good life can be...*will* be once you get past these rough times. Memories are stored treasures you can pull out to lift your spirits at any moment. Let them be a balm to your current concerns. Why make yourself crazy?

44
Don't delay your happiness.

People will fritter away their entire lives waiting to be happy. For them, happiness is always just around the corner—sure to happen when they finish school, get a job, find a spouse, have kids, get the kids out of the house, claim their inheritance, retire... You'll never be happy that way. Experience happiness now, from within, by appreciating the gifts and accomplishments you're already blessed with, rather than waiting for some elusive external event or acquisition to take place. Why make yourself crazy?

45
Don't try to know everything.

You *can't* know everything (although some may think they do). So focus on what you need to know, what you're curious to know and what will help make your life easier, happier and more productive. Don't feel pressure to learn things other people know but have little relevance to you. It's not a competition. There are probably lots of things you know that they don't, but do you hold it against *them*? Keep your quest for knowledge focused and selective. Why make yourself crazy?

46
Escape to a movie.

To a real movie. Not your TV set, not your VCR, not your DVD player. Nothing beats the undisturbed comfort and larger-than-life experience of losing yourself in a good theatrical film. And sharing the occasion with an anonymous yet likeminded audience. Few diversions are as immediately transporting and relaxing. Read reviews. Load up on your favorite movie munch. Turn off your cell phone. And take a revitalizing two-hour vacation from stress. Why make yourself crazy?

47
Don't let the media bring up your kids.

Just because it's on TV, in the movies or in a magazine doesn't make it "okay," healthy or morally acceptable. More than ever, the media are driven by ratings and profits—hardly by social responsibility. If you're stressing out over what your kids are exposed to, you should be. Sex, violence, and offensive language are being pawned off on increasingly younger audiences. Don't look the other way, claim you don't have time to be vigilant or give in because other kids are doing it. Monitor what your children watch and read very carefully. Let *your* influence—not the media's, not other parents'—guide your kids. Or risk having their childhood snatched right out from under them. Why make yourself crazy?

48
Try not to work with impatience.

Example: projects you don't have much time for... things you reluctantly have to do over...tasks you don't enjoy doing at all. If you do them impatiently—with a lack of focus, careless haste, shortness of breath—it only makes them more unpleasant, more stressful and seem longer. Do one of two things: put off the project until you're mentally prepared to take it on; or, relax and resign yourself to giving it the full attention it deserves. Once committed to doing it with patience, you might even start to enjoy the work. You have to do it anyway. Why make yourself crazy?

49
Clean out your closet.

Why start each day on a sour note by having to confront an overstuffed, messy closet? How can you possibly figure out what to wear if all your clothes are crammed in and piled up like that? Free yourself of this stifling encumbrance. Go to your local home center and get closet organizers, racks and shelves that'll help you make the most of your space. Give away what you no longer need. Enjoy the convenience of having everything sorted and easy to locate. Wake up each day feeling relaxed, organized and in control. Why make yourself crazy?

50
Ask what's involved.

Before you agree to take on a responsibility, sign up for a program or volunteer your time, determine the full extent of what's involved. It's only reasonable to ask questions up front and withhold your participation until you've had time to evaluate your role. This may save you a lot of regret later on. Don't be so quick to jump into the water before you know how deep it is. Why make yourself crazy?

51
Complete those half-finished projects.

You know, those works-in-progress you started enthusiastically but have since abandoned to lost interest or lack of time. The ones that are cluttering up your dining room table, bedroom floor, garage, backyard, den, and other living spaces. Either finish them, haul them out of sight or scuttle them altogether. They're constant, nettling reminders of a failure to get it done. And they're getting in everyone's way! Next time you start something, be sure you have the time and resolve to finish it. And enjoy the stress-releasing contentment of a project completed. Why make yourself crazy?

52
Don't sweat it if you don't
click with someone.

Very often—even though there's no animosity between you; indeed there's politeness and respect—you just don't hit it off with another person. Your understanding of each other, your senses of humor, your styles of communicating...are out of whack. Even awkward at times. These are usually people you're thrown together with by circumstance rather than choice: a coworker, a roommate, an in-law. Don't let it distress you. Many people are on different wave-lengths. And even though the both of you would like to have a more intimate relationship, it may not be in the cards. So don't force it. Just relax and try to make the best of your interactions with each other. Eventually you may find some common ground, or share an experience, that will bring you closer. Why make yourself crazy?

53
Sing along with a musical instrument.

Can't play a musical instrument? Learn one. Can't sing? Don't worry, no one else need hear. But a soothing way to chill out and release tension is to grab a guitar, or sit down at a keyboard, and accompany yourself to some favorite tunes. It should not be forced practice. And the object is not to become an accomplished musician or a skilled vocalist (although it could certainly happen). It's to enjoy the activity in itself...to let go of inhibition and express yourself musically. If you do that, you can tap into some core feelings and achieve a state of relaxed detachment. It's a groove musicians have known for centuries. And the beauty is, it's a ready escape you can have at hand almost any time you want. Why make yourself crazy?

54
Take every opportunity to walk.

Most people take every opportunity *not* to walk. And that's unfortunate. Walking delivers a wealth of physical benefits—like burning calories, exercising your heart, lungs and muscles, strengthening your immune system, and easing stress. Mentally, walking can jog ideas loose, give your mind space to think, alter your perspective, help you solve problems. All this while getting you where you want to go! Walking indeed can be the most productive use of your time. Get off your (ahem) chair, get out of your car, pick up your feet...and walk. Why make yourself crazy?

55
Toss around radical changes in your mind.

Such as, moving to another town, starting a new career, taking up a totally different kind of pastime. As extreme and unlike-you they may seem, remember, they're only scenarios in your head. It doesn't cost anything to try them on, see how they fit, and no one else need know. Every time you revisit them, they'll become a little less scary and slightly more doable. Use your imagination to break out of hemmed-in, intransigent perspectives. It could be the precursor to real change and an extraordinarily better life for you. Go ahead, fantasize. It's *free*. Why make yourself crazy?

56
Get out and socialize.

Tear yourself away from the total immersion of your work and spend some diverting wind-down time with family, friends and associates. The harder it is to do, the more you need to do it. Periodic disengagement replenishes energy and sparks ideas, lets you step back and see what direction you're headed, alerts you if you're being too single-minded. This is not a luxury, it's a necessity. And try not to bring your travails along with you. The more you get lost in your diversion, the greater the benefits will be. Get out, have fun and be a heck of a lot better off for it. Why make yourself crazy?

57
Confront your real, hidden motives.

Today, we're layers of excuses and justifications removed from the real reasons we act and feel the way do. What is the *real* reason you're angry with a loved one? You resent a neighbor or coworker? You over-schedule your life? You need to keep acquiring things? You want to win so badly? Be honest, look beneath your apparent motives and cut to the truth. You may find pride, envy, guilt, or insecurity lurking beneath. And once you acknowledge it, you can start to curb the stressful drives, or defuse the combustible situations, these feelings create. Come clean with your motives. The last person you need to fool is yourself. Why make yourself crazy?

58
Don't be the martyr.

You may think there's something noble and courageous in working excessively, missing meals, losing sleep, failing to exercise, depriving yourself of leisure, and basically running yourself into the ground. In fact, some industries and organizations actually glamorize this sort of destructive work ethic. Don't fall for it. In an emergency situation, yes, extraordinary effort may be briefly required. But every day? You're not doing yourself or your family any good by trashing your health and mental well-being. Stop playing the embattled warrior chasing after shortsighted gratification. If you want to be a hero, stay fit, eat healthy, live sensibly...and be happily more successful over the long haul. Why make yourself crazy?

59
Don't wait for someone else
to take care of it.

You may be waiting a long time. Never assume someone else will report the power outage to the utility company, file a complaint against a deceitful business, call an ambulance after an accident, report a suspicious person lurking in the neighborhood. *You* do it! You won't have that nagging feeling that nothing is being done. Even if you're not the first, the multiple reports will prompt a faster, more serious response. If you really want action, don't leave it up to others. Why make yourself crazy?

60
Don't fall victim to a chronic talker.

It's polite to hear someone out for a reasonable length of time. But if a person is hogging the conversation at a dinner party, chewing your ear off at work, or simply isn't interested in what anyone else has to say...you have every right to cut them short. Chronic yakkers will numb your brain, steal your time, chill a convivial mood, and stress you out. So interrupt. Bring others into the conversation. Or simply excuse yourself and leave. If this sends a message, so much the better. Insensitive people don't understand subtlety.

Give one-sided conversationalists the hook. Why make yourself crazy?

61
Don't expect gratitude.

You may get it, but don't expect it. Accept that a lot of your good efforts will go unacknowledged. (And your kids will never fully appreciate you until they have children of their own!) Today, people mostly take notice when things go wrong...and take the rest for granted. So rather than repeatedly set yourself up for disappointment, don't expect accolades. Do it because it's right, because it pleases *you*, because your reward should derive from the fruit of your labors, not the arbitrary whim of disinterested recipients. And when that infrequent expression of thanks does come your way, it will be that much sweeter. Why make yourself crazy?

62
Don't expect justice.

Like gratitude you may get it, but don't expect it. The world is rife with injustices, big and small. For as many people who are brought to justice, many more get away with something. Disheartening, yes. Hopeless, no. You should always seek and strive for justice. The mere act of pursuing it can help relieve the hurt and stress of being wronged, regardless of the outcome. And take comfort in knowing that at some point, somewhere, though maybe not in this life, justice *will* be served. Why make yourself crazy?

63
Be on time.

Lateness can signal a lack of respect for those you keep waiting. At least, that's how they might view it. However acceptable you think lateness has become, you can bet it still grates on those whose time is compromised. Aside from that, constantly running late is a stress factory. It'll fry your nerves, make you prone to errors and accidents, weaken your immune system, age you prematurely. Get hooked on the relaxed, liberating feeling of being ahead of schedule. All it takes is planning, practice and empathy for others. Everyone wins when you're on time. Why make yourself crazy?

64
Start on time.

If you're conducting a meeting, practice, class, seminar, presentation, or other scheduled event, begin promptly at the designated time. Waiting for people to drift in at their leisure only condones their lateness, penalizes those who made the effort to arrive punctually and sends the message it's okay to be late again next time. Start with a less important part of your program, but at least have something going so the latecomers know they're late. And don't backtrack on their account. Why throw off your schedule, and everyone else's, to accommodate an inconsiderate few? Why make yourself crazy?

65
Do menial things ordinarily done for you.

Every now and then perform some good, tough, manual tasks. Grow a salad, paint your house, rake the yard, change your car's oil, wash your clothes by hand, chop your own firewood, catch a fish for dinner, make soups and baked goods from scratch. You'll experience a primal satisfaction in meeting basic needs that our over-pampering society now shields us from. The physical exertion will also reduce your stress. And you'll appreciate more how good you really have it. So roll up your sleeves, get your hands dirty and experience the gritty joy of life the way it used to be. Why make yourself crazy?

66
Tell people what you expect of them.

How else are they going to know what you want? And how to deliver it? When you're the boss, the customer, the parent, the teacher...you can't be vague or timid. You have to be clear, firm and decisive. Don't be shy about giving orders or afraid you'll ruffle some feathers. People are looking to you for direction. They want it. And you have every right, indeed obligation, to give it. You can save yourself and others a lot of frustration when you simply take command and let them know what you expect. Why make yourself crazy?

67
Be a slug one day a week.

Especially if you're a jackrabbit the other six. Sleep late. Languish in bed with the newspapers. Don't answer the phone. Go out for brunch. It's okay. It's not a crime. In fact, considering how you normally abuse yourself, it's downright virtuous. Even better, designate a day the whole family can be slugs. No shuttling the kids around frantically. No social calendar to be slave to. Just let things happen...lazily and naturally. It will leave you more energized and better prepared to tackle the week ahead. Why make yourself crazy?

68
Channel your anger into productive energy.

Anger is like steam. Held in, it can build to the point of bursting, leaving damage in its wake. But also like steam, which can propel an engine, you can release your anger in positive ways. Make a conscious effort not to dwell or feed on it. Instead, get busy. Channel your anger into rational and composed ways to deal with the problem that caused it. You'll be more likely to dispel it peacefully, rather than pop off in a manner you might regret. Why make yourself crazy?

69
Smile at people.

Note how you feel next time someone smiles at you. Probably welcome, cheered, confident, warm, appreciated. That's the power you have to make others feel, simply by smiling at them. A smile can instantly disarm a bad mood, ease a tense relationship, persuade another to cooperate, initiate a friendship. And you always have this potent tool at your disposal. When you smile, studies have shown, good things happen to you, too. You become more relaxed and cheerful. Not to mention the positive vibes you'll get from reciprocated smiles. Too serious and grim-faced? Wear an occasional smile. Why make yourself crazy?

70
Cooking is a microcosm of life.

It involves on a smaller scale a lot of the same skills and attitudes we need to survive out in the world. For example, a meal has to be thought out beforehand, so it requires good planning skills. Ingredients have to be purchased, calling for knowledge, judgment and economy. Artistic ability comes into play in the meal's makeup and presentation. Most importantly, everything must be orchestrated to be completed within a reasonable timeframe. Finally, it should all be done in a spirit of conviviality and graciousness. If you can master the challenges of cooking, you'll be more than rewarded with great meals... you'll develop the skills to succeed at pretty much everything else. Why make yourself crazy?

71
Keep meetings short and sweet.

Meetings are great tools for focusing in on objectives, assigning tasks, measuring progress, motivating a group. They can also be horrendous time wasters. Don't schedule a meeting unless you have ample reason to justify one. Have an agenda and stick to it. Don't let others digress, or use it as a platform to showcase their speaking abilities. Stagger the arrival and departure of those who needn't be there the entire time. And enjoy fewer, more productive, anxiety-free meetings. Why make yourself crazy?

72
Got freedom? Use it.

Don't just take it for granted. Or merely acknowledge it. Use it. Freedom is like an all-purpose tool. You can accomplish an extraordinary amount of things with it. Because you're free to do, speak and move about as you wish. To change things. To seek knowledge and wisdom. To make your world a safer, happier, less stressful place. What a waste of unused potential if you don't take full advantage of that! In a free society, you've got the green light to progress in just about any direction you choose. The opportunities are boundless. Think about that next time you feel oppressed—a prisoner of your circumstances. You don't have to accept it. You've got freedom. And you'll never feel more empowered, more in control of your destiny, than when you start putting it to use. Why make yourself crazy?

73
Stop and think.

It's amazing how much time, money and trouble we could save ourselves if we just took the time to think before we acted. Next time you feel compelled to dash into something, pause a moment. Run possible scenarios in your mind. Weigh consequences. Consider alternatives. Ask more questions. Or just think it through. You'll be surprised at how often you'll overrule your initial rushed impulses and find a better way. Just by taking the time to think. Your mind is the most efficient tool you have. Use it. Why make yourself crazy?

74
Don't answer your morning emails right away.

Read them, but don't answer them—unless there's an immediate fire to put out. They'll sap your time and the mental energy needed for more important tasks. Save them for later when you need a break. Responding will be easier then, too, since your subconscious will be working on them all the while. (Notice how you instantly know what to say when you revisit them.) Personal messages and jokes can be especially insidious and take a big chunk out of your day. They're like electronic water coolers. And try not to interrupt your workflow every time a new message arrives. Wait till you've got a bunch. The object here: fewer distractions, more focus, less stress. Why make yourself crazy?

75
Welcome to the age of exploitation.

This is an era where people are gratuitously exploited, abused, tormented, humiliated, then tossed away like used tissues. And that's just on TV! The reality-show ethic has spilled over into the real world, or is it the other way around? Regardless, it seems that tolerance for one's mistakes, caring for another's feelings, and treating people with respect and dignity have gone out the window. Unless there's something in it for someone. As a society, we must ask ourselves: Whom do we really care about? Who really cares about us—beyond affected concern, beyond having a stake in us? This intolerance for error, relentless pursuit of self-interest, and readiness to heap scorn on fellow human beings creates enormous distrust and friction among us. Think about how much you've become a part of this...and how much better things might be if you weren't. Why make yourself crazy?

76
Make the "I'm running
late" phone call.

When it's fairly certain you're not going to arrive on time...make the call. Let others know in advance you'll be delayed. It accomplishes several things. You'll experience an immediate unburdening of stress and a sense of relief. You won't be keeping people hanging, fuming and wondering where you are. Your alert will allow them to alter their plans accordingly. And by the time you do arrive, they will have appreciated your courtesy, adjusted to the situation and be more agreeable with you. So don't just arrive way overdue and try to minimize it with a trite "Sorry I'm late." Call ahead and let them know you're delayed. Why make yourself crazy?

77
Don't rely on litigation.

Who among us does not at least once a day sue another person or entity in the courtroom of our mind? And how brilliantly these imagined legal battles always play out in our favor! We'll fix them! Forget about it. Like back surgery, avoid litigation at all costs. Negotiate. Compromise. Work out an agreement. Or back off. But the last thing you want is to bring out the lawyers, haul in the witnesses and spend years of agony and stress dragging an issue through the court system. Nobody wins. So don't view litigation as your ace in the hole, your insurance policy against bad dealings and unsettled disputes. It's a quagmire. Unless it's an absolute necessity, you don't want to go there. Why make yourself crazy?

78
Don't let them get away with it.

The reason why customer service is so abominable today is that people just accept it. The company usually doesn't care as long as they're raking it in. And granted, who wants to play menu tag or wait on hold half an hour to grouse at a low-level functionary? But you know what? It's more aggravating to do nothing. Because every time you think about it you're going to seethe. And that's not good. So take a few minutes and write an email complaint. To give it some oomph, copy any consumer organizations, industry associations or government agencies you think might stick in the offender's craw. Then shoot it off. If it goes unanswered, dump the chumps. If you get a reply, you've scored some points. Either way, take some satisfaction in not letting them get away with it. You hold the ultimate buying decision. Why make yourself crazy?

79
Heed the counsel of wisdom.

The wiser you are about how the world works...
the true nature of people and their motives...the
pitfalls, traps and dead-ends that lie in wait—the
less stressful your life will be. Wisdom is more
than the accumulation of knowledge. It's the ability
to take what you've learned, see things as they are
and act accordingly—with sound judgment and
prudence. Wisdom can hit you like a knock on the
head (for example, when you make a glaring mistake), or reveal itself through intelligent thought
and deliberation. (The latter is more preferable.) Either way, heed its message. Stand aside, utilize the
objective vantage point that wisdom affords you,
and the choices you make can't help but be better
ones. Why make yourself crazy?

80
Do you stress out in social situations?

Are you uncomfortable mingling at a party? Do
you fear whatever you say will be trite and uninter-
esting? Do you feel conspicuous and ill at ease?
This can be perfectly normal, especially if it's people
you don't know in an unfamiliar setting. Fretting
about it will only add to your angst. When you're in

an "I don't know anyone!" state, try turning the tables. Assume others are feeling out of place and it's your job to make them comfortable. This will take the focus off you, give you reason to initiate contact and allow you to show an interest in someone else, an admirable social grace. Do this soon after you arrive so the tension of having to break the ice doesn't mount. It'll help you thrive in any social situation. Why make yourself crazy?

81
It ain't over until the check clears.

Always remember this: the most difficult thing to exact from another human being is money. People will subject you to the most imaginative array of excuses, promises, delays, apologies, and evasions before they ever see fit to cough up the dough. And few things are more stressful than having to wait even a second longer than necessary for the sum that is due you. So never let the allure of money impair your judgment of another's ability and willingness to pay. And never be so foolhardy as to think you're in the chips until the check has cleared and the funds are safely tucked away in your account. Why make yourself crazy?

82
Don't wear your stress like a badge.

"Look at me! Look how busy, rushed and vital I am!" This, unfortunately, is the way many of us view our overscheduled lives. Sure, running around in the thick of it can often be exhilarating. But it's a precarious house of cards. A single scheduling glitch can cause everything to spin out of control. Worse, always operating in crisis mode puts a tremendous amount of stress and wear-and-tear on you—weakening your immune system and aging you mercilessly. So don't compete or boast about how crazed you are. Being productively calm and in control wins out in the long run. Why make yourself crazy?

83
Get a pet.

If no one else will soothe you, listen to you, give you the unconditional attention you deserve, a pet certainly can. Studies have shown that pets can ease appreciably the tension and stress of those around them—almost instantaneously. What a potent antidote to your daily tribulations! Even something as tiny and maintenance-free as a tropical fish can deliver some of these benefits. If you get a pet, talk to it, dote on it, let your affectionate interaction be a salve to your daily concerns. Cat? Dog? Hamster? Parakeet? Choose the stress remedy that fits you best. Why make yourself crazy?

84
Never sacrifice safety for expediency.

It's frightening the risks people take when rushed or running late. Like driving with reckless distraction—putting their kids, themselves and others in danger. When it gets to the point where you're cutting corners, taking chances, sacrificing good judgment over mere trivial matters...alarms should go off. Slow down. Get a grip. Or one day it's going to catch up with you. Life is too short to rush through anyway. Why make yourself crazy?

85
Get into shape.

Lack of time is no excuse for not exercising. In fact, being in shape will improve your physical and mental capacity to such an extent, you'll probably *gain* time. And enjoy life more. A regular fitness routine, combined with good eating habits, will keep you leaner, healthier, more energetic. You owe that to yourself. And your family. Being in poor physical condition only adds to your stress and the sense of futility that you'll never catch up. Climb out of that swamp. Get fit. Feel good. Why make yourself crazy?

86
Don't be goaded into making hasty decisions.

If you feel unsure, or don't know enough to make a decision...*don't.* Most decisions can be put off. Wait till you have all the facts. And never be rushed into deciding by a salesperson because a "special offer" will expire. Any reputable company will extend their terms until you've at least had time to think about it—something they may not want you to do. Don't rush into anything you aren't sure of. Why make yourself crazy?

87
Play with the kids as soon as you get home.

Yes, you have a million other things to do. Or maybe you'd just like to relax. But spending time with your kids first will show them you love them above all else. It will satisfy their need to be with you and pre-empt both their nagging and your putting them off. Chances are, they'll soon get distracted anyway and go off to do something else, leaving you with time to yourself...without the guilt. Make a fuss over the kids first. Why make yourself crazy?

88
Expect people to cancel out on you.

Last-minute dropouts and no-shows can be disappointing—especially when you've gone to a lot of trouble. Blame it on our over-scheduled times, a general slackening of social responsibility, whatever. But this, unfortunately, is the way things are. So be ready for it. If you're planning an event or activity involving several people, expect one or more will almost certainly cancel. Invite or recruit extra people to make up for the inevitable loss. And if everyone does show up (slim chance), you'll enjoy an unanticipated bonus. Why make yourself crazy?

89
Speak up.

Don't know what they're talking about? Ask. Don't agree with what's being said? Speak up. Your opinion is just as valid as anyone's. And the only stupid question is the one that's not asked. People often assume we have the same prior knowledge they do, and start in the middle of things. It's not your fault; it's theirs. So don't be shy. Before it goes any further, interrupt.

Tell them to backtrack a bit. Ask basic questions. And get up to speed. Why make yourself crazy?

90
Run through it again.

Don't always assume another person is on the same page as you are. Or fully understands what the program is. Repeat the instructions, go through the itinerary once again, ask that phone numbers and directions be read back to you. Better to be redundant, or a pain in the butt, than have everything screwed up altogether. Run through it one last time. Why make yourself crazy?

91
Take ten minutes a day to neaten up.

Supplement your regularly scheduled cleaning by spending a short time each day neatening your home. Use those few minutes to clear a cluttered surface, tidy a child's room, clean out a drawer, throw out a useless item or two, dust a long forgotten place, put something away...or whatever obvious need is staring you in the face. You'll be amazed at how much this small attention to neatness can accomplish over time. And how organized and productive you'll become. And when you do get around to more intense cleaning, the job will be that much easier. Take ten minutes a day to tidy up. Why make yourself crazy?

92
Don't leave yourself in the dark.

Fear is often driven by lack of information. We're afraid of what we don't know, or what we might find out. But not knowing just prolongs the anxiety and runs you down both physically and mentally, interfering with everything you do. And it's certainly not going to alter the truth, good or bad. For these reasons it's almost always better to know. Get to the bottom of what's bothering you...so you can deal with it and move on. Ask questions. Be informed. Why make yourself crazy?

93
Work before play.

Leisure is better enjoyed when it follows a period of good hard work. But putting off work to have your fun first is another story. Rather than relieving stress, it can be a source of it. Because now you made a conscious decision to fall behind. And the prospect of neglected work to make up can erode your fun. Don't let others lure you away from your appointed tasks, either. (Dereliction loves company.) Students are especially vulnerable to this. In the work/play cycle the effort should always come first, before the reward. Why make yourself crazy?

94
Beat the heat.

When the weather turns hot, your level of stress rises right along with it. And the more you think about how uncomfortable you are, how dragged out you feel, how devilishly torrid it is...the more impatient, stifled and irritable you become. Which doesn't help the situation. When the temperature climbs, it's time to scale back your intensity relative to the heat so you can function effectively without boiling over or burning out. Also essential: drink plenty of cold water. Think cool thoughts. Stay out of the sun. And don't bring attention to your discomfort, either to yourself or others. It's a heat wave. Accept it. Adapt to it. Then ride it out. Why make yourself crazy?

95
An ego is the hardest
thing to maintain.

Egotism is addictive. The more you feed it, the more it needs to be fed. If your self-worth is dependent on the adulation of others, you put yourself at their mercy, and they may not always be willing to comply. People are notoriously fickle. They love creating icons so they can gleefully knock them off their pedestals. Think about that. No matter how rich or famous you are, if your self-esteem needs endless coddling you become nothing but a slave to it...and have to constantly work, stress and even pander to maintain it. Look at all the self-anointed pooh-bahs of the world falling all over themselves for the slightest recognition. Do you admire them? Or snigger at their almost childlike appetite for attention? The opposite of this is altruism. Do good for the simple joy of doing good. If praise comes your way, fine. If it doesn't, that's okay, too. Why make yourself crazy?

96
Live proactively, not reactively.

The reason people under constant stress feel so unfulfilled, despite their ceaseless activity, is that they've lost control. They aren't calling the shots anymore. Reeling from crisis to crisis, at the mercy of circumstances, unable to catch up and regain the initiative. If this kind of rudderless existence is dogging you, you have to reassert control. That means: stop reacting and start doing things in a more proactive, planned and orderly way. If you doubt this is a better approach, consider that you'll experience fewer mishaps and mistakes, much less energy wasted on stress and anxiety, greater efficiency, more satisfaction, even a boost in productivity. So dig in your heels, take over the controls and get your life back on track. Why make yourself crazy?

97
Create a garden.

Why do so many people around the world resort to gardening to escape the rigors and pressures of their day jobs? And swear by it? For one, it brings you back to earth. Literally. It fosters nurturing, caring and growth. You can't rush it (thankfully). It involves good physical effort. You see the results of that effort. You can take pride in it. And create something of beauty and value. It's life the way it once was, before it became drowned in complexity. It's instinctive. So if you're looking for the antithesis of what you do now, go green. Create a garden. Start small and build. Don't have available land? Do it indoors, with potted plants and imaginative interior landscapes. It may be new, alien and unfamiliar to you. But that's part of the appeal. Why make yourself crazy?

98
Cook enough for several meals.

Why go to all the trouble to shop for ingredients, prepare the food, cook it, and clean everything up... for a single meal? Double or triple the amount of the dish you're making and freeze the rest for later. The marginal increase in work will more than pay for itself on those bedraggled evenings when you can pop a delicious dinner in the microwave, sit back and unwind. Prepare more now, toil less later. Why make yourself crazy?

99
Don't always expect government to cure your ills.

If you're depending on government to right every wrong that befalls you, you're in for some frustrating times ahead. Because we pay so much in taxes, we expect to get top-notch services in return. And as you're well aware, that's not always the case. (In some quarters, *rarely* the case.) Government was never meant to replace self-reliance and personal responsibility anyway. The services it performs best are those aimed at the collective good rather than individual need. When you have a problem, you have every right to call on your local representative or the appropriate agency to help solve it. But don't be surprised if it's met with red tape, lack of interest, delays, and denials. So rather than grind your teeth down at night, be prepared to deal with the issue in other ways. Why make yourself crazy?

100
Do more things *live.*

Are you living life through the pixilated gauze of a computer screen? Are your conversations with others conducted mostly by keyboard? Does your travel consist of looking at photographs in a magazine? Are your adventures played out vicariously on a game console? Are you more familiar with TV characters than your own neighbors? As ingenious as technology may be, it can't replace flesh and blood, fresh air, natural sights, sounds, smells, and physical activity. And you need that. More than you think. Constantly living one step removed from reality, you can easily lose touch with it. And fall victim to the stress, anxiety and isolation of physical detachment. You've got to get out more. Be with real people, see real things, experience live events. There's no substitute. Why make yourself crazy?

101
Change your thinking patterns.

Ingrained negative thoughts and stock reactions often perpetuate the cycle of stress and anxiety. They sabotage any chance at peace and enjoyment. Example: you react with fear every time a new project is assigned to you—even though you're competent and successful! Or you treat like a calamity even the tiniest mishap or delay. Or take what's merely a helpful suggestion as a stinging criticism. First, listen to what you're thinking at these moments. Then consciously dispute any unwarranted reaction or overreaction. Notice how these incidents don't amount to anything when they happen to others. So why let them bedevil you? A lot of unjustified reactions are carryovers from childhood. They have no logical place in your life today. You have to identify and dismantle them over time. Why make yourself crazy?

102
Don't let advertisers make you feel inadequate.

Companies spend billions each year to convince us we're tasteless, uncouth, unsanitary, out of touch, incomplete bumpkins if we don't use their products or services. If anyone has to resort to those tactics, it's likely you don't need the item to begin with, much less the insults that go with it. In fact, when an ad attempts to make you feel lacking, you should make a point NOT to buy it. It'll give you a feeling of empowerment, and free you from the stress of chasing after yet another contrived need. Don't let profit-motivated advertisers shame you into purchasing their products. Buy on true need alone. Why make yourself crazy?

103
Become a fan.

Root for something. Or someone. A sports team, a star athlete, a celebrity idol. A person facing a daunting challenge. Or someone trying to accomplish a feat that's never been done. Maybe even (dare I say?) a politician. Whatever, whomever—whether local, national or international—being a fan is known to reduce stress. Yes, it's true. In spite of the fact you'll pull your hair out over bonehead plays, lackluster performance and heartbreaking defeats. Or perhaps *because* of it. Screaming at the TV or stomping your feet in the grandstand is certainly a way to release tension. So pick out your heroes and throw your support behind them. Follow their progress. Attend their performances. Deck yourself out in their gear.

And see what mitigating effect it has on your stress. Why make yourself crazy?

104
Don't assume others don't have problems.

Why can't our lives be as smooth, relaxed and problem-free as other people's seem to be? That's the deceptive picture we often view through the prism of our own crazed existence. Don't believe it for an instant. Almost everyone today is feeling the pressure of our high-expectation society, dealing with the same ridiculous schedules and excessive responsibilities you are. They just don't care to show it. (How often do *you* reply "great" when others ask how it's going?) Not that we wish a frazzled life on anyone. But knowing it's fairly widespread helps to reduce your own anxiety level. Don't despair. You're not alone. Why make yourself crazy?

105
Give back.

In an era when it seems the primary endeavor of mankind is to take, how refreshing and liberating it is to give back! And not just to respond to another's need because you happen to be around at the time, but to go out of your way to volunteer your time and energy to charitable or community projects. When you expose yourself to the reality of what others have to endure, your problems pale in comparison. You've been fortunate. It's time to give a little back, gain some needed perspective and feel really good about yourself in doing it. Why make yourself crazy?

106
Tell the salesperson you're shopping around.

Whether buying a car, insurance, windows, stereo system, condo...any big item that involves a salesperson...tell the rep right off you're comparison shopping and they're the first you've contacted. This informs them at the outset you won't be making a decision that day. It's your escape hatch, avoiding the mounting stress and awkwardness of having to wriggle your way out at the end of a lengthy sales pitch. It also tests the sincerity of the salesperson, who's attitude toward you might change noticeably if an immediate sale isn't in the offing. You'll be in a better negotiating position, too, since they know they'll have to compete. And if they still try to pressure you into signing, vowing that you won't find a better deal elsewhere, simply assure them that if it's true, they have nothing to worry about. Why make yourself crazy?

107
Try to be positive for an entire day.

For one day, experience what it would be like to banish negativity from your entire life. Every time bad feelings, lack of confidence and discouragement start to creep in, quash them with positive thoughts and actions. Rather than bemoan your fate, turn mishaps into opportunities, mistakes into learning experiences. There's a positive aspect to every situation, and it's up to you to find it. And the way you react will have a major impact on making things better or worse. Today—all day—replace negative thoughts and attitudes with confidence and optimism. Why make yourself crazy?

108
Don't be a rushed and restless driver.

If you often have an urge to drive over the car in front of you...become exasperated at even the slightest traffic tie-up...get annoyed with others who are merely driving safely...and incessantly speed up only to slow down...you need to get a grip. You've forgotten that driving is a convenience, not an inconvenience. And in your impatience, you're prematurely aging your car and, more importantly, yourself. Step back a bit. Be grateful you've got a car to get you there in the first place. And adapt to the realities of driving. Leave yourself extra time, relax behind the wheel, benefit from the transition time, and enjoy the ride. Why make yourself crazy?

109
Spend time near the water.

Whether it's a stroll along the river, eating lunch by a pond in the park, weekending at a scenic lake, or vacationing by the sea...the mere sight and presence of water is a wonderful balm to the stressed-out soul. Let its naturally soothing effects ease your concerns and freshen your outlook. Let its shimmering expanse free you of the narrowed perspective of a frenzied routine. If, like most people, you're drawn to water, follow those instincts. It's nature's very own tranquilizer. Why make yourself crazy?

110
Use the proper tools.

Nothing can get the job done better, faster, safer, and ultimately more economically than the right tool. Buy, rent or borrow, but make sure you avail yourself of the benefits and time-saving convenience of quality tools. Take the time to read instructions and learn how to use them properly and safely. Renting can be cheaper in the short run, but buying often doesn't cost that much more and you won't have to rush through the task. And you'll almost certainly use that tool again...and again. Get it done like a pro. Why make yourself crazy?

111
Be a kid again.

For many of us, life consists of two phases. Experiencing childhood. And spending the rest of our lives trying to recapture it. The problem is, we mistakenly pursue the dreams we had as children (which can often be unachievable or unfulfilling), rather than revisiting the carefree life we actually lived. So if you want to feel like a kid again, chasing after expensive "toys" and vain fantasies is not the way to go. Instead, live simply, laugh a lot, work at what you love, be spontaneous, eat animal crackers, and do fun things with your family and friends. Why make yourself crazy?

112
Acknowledge your good fortune, too.

It always seems the breaks go against us: a cancelled flight, an untimely ailment, a traffic tie-up, a bad call by the referee, a rained-out event. The reason we feel cheated is, we fail to give due credit when the breaks go our way. Next time things unexpectedly work out for you, make a mental note of it. Then, when your luck turns sour, use it as a reminder that it all evens out in the long run. In fact, you might even make the philosophical leap that life itself is a stroke of good fortune and the bad breaks are merely glitches. Why make yourself crazy?

113
Don't let rushing be your default response.

We're so often pressured and hurried, rushing has become a way of life. Even when there's no need for it! Always operating in crisis mode puts tremendous stress on your nerves and immune system—creating excess levels of harmful stress hormones and free radicals that contribute to disease and aging. Break this destructive habit. When there's no reason to rush, don't. Condition yourself to do things in a sure, composed manner. You'll be more efficient, make fewer mistakes, stay a lot healthier, and live a lot longer. Who can argue that? Why make yourself crazy?

114
Get more out of life by doing less.

What a concept! Is your life fulfilling? Or is it merely crammed? Know the difference and you'll realize it's not the quantity of activities you engage in (or possessions you collect) that ultimately determine your happiness. One naturally unfolding, enriching experience can easily surpass many rushed and distracted ones. But you may be so chronically overscheduled, you never give yourself a chance to enjoy anything to the fullest. Experiment. Choose an occasion and give it your complete, mindful and unhurried attention. Then imagine an entire life of such enrichment. It's absolutely attainable. Why make yourself crazy?

115
Don't assume the responsibilities of others.

It's one thing to help someone who is genuinely in need. It's quite another to take on the responsibilities of people who are perfectly capable of discharging them themselves. You're not doing anyone a favor by letting them off the hook. And you're piling more unneeded stress and resentment on yourself. So next time you're thinking about giving your children, coworkers, friends, hirelings, and others a free ride, think again. It's their responsibility, not yours. Why make yourself crazy?

116
Don't get all worked up over little things.

Like a late charge for a payment you made on time...not being enrolled in a program you signed up for...a no-show appointment...a package that doesn't arrive...an article left behind. Your initial reaction might be one of outrage, injustice, exasperation. Mostly because now you have to find out what went wrong and correct it—on top of everything else you have to do. Stay calm. Expect to be blindsided by these unpleasant little surprises...and roll with them. You'll find that things are rarely as bad as your initial reaction to them. And often have a perfectly rational explanation...or a simple solution. Why make yourself crazy?

117
Work on your weaknesses.

Everyone tends to build on their strengths. And for good reason. It's easier and more immediately productive. The problem is, it ignores your weaknesses. And real strength comes when you work on those. It takes blunt honesty to admit you've got them in the first place. And courage to meet them head on. (If it was easy, they wouldn't be called weaknesses.) Identify your frailties. And shore them up. You'll become a more complete, balanced, respected person...and live a fuller, less stressful life. Why make yourself crazy?

118
Speak clearly and deliberately.

Avoid these barriers to good communication: rushing your words to the point where they lose their meaning or effectiveness; talking around a problem rather than getting to the point; unnecessarily repeating yourself or saying far more than you need to. Instead, choose your words carefully, *take the time* to express yourself clearly and distinctly, and speak with directness and honesty. If another tries to step on your words, or steer you in another direction, calmly hold your ground until your point is made. You listen to others. It's only right they listen to you. Why make yourself crazy?

119
Engage in a sport.

If you don't already, it's an excellent way to exercise, relieve stress, socialize, and have fun...all at the same time. It also satisfies a need for competition—healthy competition—either against yourself (like golf), or others (tennis or softball). As our lives grow busier and more complicated, we eliminate active play. And that's a mistake. Even if you've never considered yourself much of an athlete, you can likely find an enjoyable sport that matches your ability and intensity level. Just make the effort. Whether it's basketball, volleyball, racquetball, or croquet, don't deny yourself the inexpressible release of being totally absorbed in a game. Why make yourself crazy?

120
Don't let your marriage become a lifelong feud.

Marriage isn't a competition to see whose ways and viewpoints ultimately win out. If you take that attitude—always trying to prove you're right and the other is wrong—expect a life of tension and discord. Instead, *welcome* your partner's input and perspective, work together to achieve goals and know when it's more important to back off than get your way. (How would *you* like to lose all the time?) View marriage as sharing—not hoarding—and your days are sure to be happier and more stress-free. Why make yourself crazy?

121
Maintain your presence of mind.

It's easy to get flustered, panic and lose your composure when you're rushed and pressured. Your mistake level soars, carelessness abounds and civility often goes out the window. Only making things worse. Practice maintaining your presence of mind in pressure situations. Take slow deep breaths and approach the crisis with calmness and control. You'll discover you can handle things more efficiently, even more quickly, when you strive to keep your cool. Hysteria accomplishes nothing. Why make yourself crazy?

122
If you don't want to answer
the phone...don't.

There's no law or rule of etiquette that says you have to drop what you're doing, interrupt a meal, lose your train of thought, or miss your favorite show...to answer the telephone. Unless of course you want to. If not, screen your calls with caller ID. Or let your voice mail pick it up. There are few things that can't wait until you're available to talk. And you certainly don't want to be waylaid by an endless yapper at an inopportune time. Busy? Let the phone ring. Why make yourself crazy?

123
Note where you set things down.

Make a deliberate mental snapshot of where you temporarily put that pen, tool, pair of reading glasses, or piece of paper. Not easy, since it's usually a distraction that made you set it down in the first place. But after a few tries you'll get a knack for remembering where it is. Also, avoid bringing a tool you're working with away from the work area. It will usually be unwittingly left behind. This can save you hours of search time over a year. Why make yourself crazy?

124
View paying bills as a
positive experience.

This may be a real stretch for many, since bills can be a great source of aggravation, fear and anxiety. But it doesn't have to be that way. Rather than receive your invoices with dread, let them be reminders of what you're paying for: products that improve your life, services that keep you safe and comfortable, good times you've enjoyed. Be thankful when you have the funds to satisfy your obligations and view these payments as accomplishments, not "diminishments." Look at a bill paid as a transaction resolved, a milestone reached, a responsibility met. Why make yourself crazy?

125
Prepare for tomorrow...tonight.

Why wait till the last frantic minute to pick out your clothes, do needed ironing, set the breakfast table, shine your shoes, prepare the kids' lunches, and gather what you'll need for work? Take 15 or 20 minutes and do it this evening, when you're calm, unhurried and less likely to err or forget. You'll not only sleep better knowing you're ready, you'll spare yourself a lot of excess stress in the morning. Do it tonight. Why make yourself crazy?

126
Don't be reluctant to take
a contrary position.

Most conflicts, driven by pride, are unnecessary and avoidable. Those who recognize this can generally glide through life without the snags and entanglements many people get hung up on. But there are times when you simply have to take a stand, when silence or inaction will eat away at your peace of mind, or worse, your ability to function normally. In such cases take action, speak up, make your disapproval known. And don't fear being branded a dissident, especially if you rarely dissent. In fact, it will make your opposition all the more forceful. Know when it's best to go against. Why make yourself crazy?

127
Leave yourself an extra day at the end of your vacation.

Enjoy a day of transition at home to unpack, read your mail, do your laundry, reconnect with others, catch up on things, or simply relax...before heading back to work. Thrusting yourself right into your busy routine without a breather is asking for the same stress you were trying to escape in the first place. That extra day of reentry and re-acclimation can make a huge difference. Take it. Why make yourself crazy?

128
Tell them you'll get back to them.

When people ask you point blank to do something—like volunteer, go on a date, buy something, change your schedule, do them a favor, or donate money—don't feel you have to answer right away. Even if they pressure you to do so. Surprise tactics aren't fair. And could force you to commit to something you'll later regret. Tell them: "I have to think about it." Or, "I'll get back to you." Or, "I need to check on something first." If that doesn't satisfy them, decline altogether.

Being too accommodating is probably what has you stressed out in the first place. It's time you looked out for yourself. Why make yourself crazy?

129
Stop trying to change people.

People basically are what they are. A grouch will usually remain a grouch, a loud laugher a loud laugher, a pushover a pushover, a tacky person a tacky person. If any change is going to happen, it has to come from *you*—changing your belief you can make someone something they're not. Miraculous influence does occasionally happen, but mostly in the movies. So stop agonizing over a failure to mold someone into your ideal. Accept who they are and will always be. Why make yourself crazy?

130
Minimize the stress of buying a car.

Purchasing a new automobile should be an exciting and pleasant experience. Unfortunately, many car dealers make it an anxiety-fraught and unsavory one. Even if you fancy yourself a car-savvy person, you'll still be outnumbered, overmatched and subjected to the well-honed sales tactics of shrewd professionals. Be ready. Arm yourself with consumer research and price data (widely available on the Web). Never accept an offer until you've had at least a day to analyze it, think it over and comparison shop. And don't thrash out a good deal only to give it back by succumbing to worthless dealer add-ons. Be tough, deal firmly. Why make yourself crazy?

131
Don't be a slave to your image.

How much unnecessary stress, excessive work and lost time with loved ones do you incur in the name of how you look to others? Are where you live, what you drive, how you dress, whom you socialize with, and where you send your kids to school dictated more by what's best for you and your family...or by the image you want to project? Carefully scrutinize your motives. You may find that a simpler lifestyle within your means might leave you with less of what impresses others...but more of what makes your life easier, happier and more fulfilling. Why make yourself crazy?

132
Put the kids to work.

For many children, life is a posh resort, every need fulfilled, parents waiting on them hand and foot. Okay when they're very young, foolish when they're old enough to take on responsibility...and take some of the burden off you. Love them, but don't spoil them. Assign chores and projects commensurate with their age (making beds, clearing the table, vacuuming the floor, taking the garbage out). Pay them for extra, non-routine work like washing the car or pulling weeds. And don't be so quick to step in for them when they start to whine or balk. Toughing it out builds character. They win. You win. Why make yourself crazy?

133
Don't be rushed by people behind you.

It always seems the person in back of you on line, on the road or on the golf course is in a hurry, impatient, intolerant of the slightest delay. Don't let it get to you. When in line, take time to take care of your needs properly. Don't be distracted or rushed into losing your focus or making costly mistakes. You were first, you're in front, they can wait. On the road, resist being goaded into driving unsafely (let the speeders and road hogs pass if they can). And don't let another's rudeness on the golf course ruin your game. It's not the Masters. It's supposed to be fun. Why make yourself crazy?

134
Meditate.

Close your eyes, relax your entire body and get in touch with your inner self. It's easy, doesn't take much time and can melt away your stress like a summer breeze. There are many ways to meditate and just as many books on the subject. Whatever approach you take, the idea is simple: a calming respite that can put your mind, body and soul back into sync. Set aside at least twenty minutes each day to meditate. Why make yourself crazy?

135
Invite someone over for coffee.

Or tea, or a glass of wine, or a beer, if that's your preference. Somehow this simple and relaxing way to connect with others has lost ground to more elaborate and expensive forms of entertaining. Or maybe you just can't seem to find the time any- more. But simple drop-by visits with friends and neighbors is a great way to catch up, share experi- ences, vent concerns, and give yourself a needed break from the rat race. Pure, uplifting social in- teraction...without all the fuss. Try it. Why make yourself crazy?

136
Don't be driven to Internet distraction.

The Web can soak up precious time so insidiously you're often not even aware of it. How easily a simple online task can end up taking an hour or more! Be smart. Devise your plan of attack before going on. And stick with it. Don't be lured away by enticing links or allow yourself to drift about aimlessly. Log on, get what you want and get off. Make the Internet the efficient, timesaving tool it was meant to be, and save your surfing for your leisure hours. Why make yourself crazy?

137
Stand up and stretch.

Especially if you have a desk or computer job. A day at work shouldn't be like an eight-hour plane ride. Periodically get off your chair and stand, stretching your arms and legs—even squatting, bending from side to side, rolling your head, walking about, etc. It'll get the blood flowing more freely, loosen cramped muscles and joints, help you think more clearly, and relieve some of the stress. Give your body a quick tune-up at least one or two minutes each hour. Why make yourself crazy?

138
Try not to attach money to self-worth.

Yes, most people do to a certain extent. After all, our self-esteem is buoyed by our achievements, and money can be a quantifiable measurement of achievement. But accumulating money for its own sake is an unquenchable pursuit that will always leave you less than fulfilled. It also diverts your attention from nobler, more selfless acts. Know the point at which trying to earn more becomes superfluous, obsessive and ultimately detrimental, and direct your efforts to worthier pursuits that offer lasting esteem and satisfaction. Why make yourself crazy?

139
Empathize.

Develop the habit of putting yourself in another person's situation. No, don't just picture it, *feel* it. Use a parallel situation in your own life, like actors do, to conjure up the poignancy of emotion another person might be experiencing. When you do this, you'll see more clearly why people act the way they do. And even if you don't agree with those actions, you'll understand them a lot better. You'll ease some of the tension and indignation you may be feeling, and be more willing to lend help rather than just disapprove. Empathy is a quality the entire world can learn and profit from. Attitudes and relationships improve dramatically when you attempt to see things from another's point of view. Why make yourself crazy?

140
Don't be so thin-skinned.

Why let an off-the-cuff remark or minor criticism rankle you to the degree it leaves you tense, angry and unable to focus on much else? Develop a hide thick enough so that verbal slights bounce right off and get only the minimal attention they deserve. (Sometimes we misconstrue what was said, too.) Overblown reactions create unnecessary stress and negative energy. To what purpose? You can bet the off-putting remark isn't bothering the person who delivered it! Don your emotional flak jacket and accept that you can't always please everyone. Why make yourself crazy?

But when it really hurts...

141
Get it off your chest immediately.

You've been grossly or ungraciously snubbed, insulted, ignored, mistreated, or misunderstood. Don't hold it in and let it fester. It can breed harmful stress and resentment, impede your ability to function, destroy an important relationship. In a composed manner, as soon as convenient, let the other party know how upset you are. Explain why you feel hurt. Ask that suitable recompense or apology be made. You may not always get the satisfaction you seek, but confronting the issue will help vent your anger and relieve some of the distress you're feeling. It also sends the message you won't tolerate such treatment in the future. When it really smarts, they need to hear from you. Why make yourself crazy?

142
Don't let others donate your services for you.

People are very generous when it comes to volunteering the services of others, especially to escape doing it themselves. ("If you need a ride to the airport, my wife will be happy to drive you!") As a result, you suddenly find yourself strapped with onerous tasks and obligations you can ill afford to take on...all liberally extended without your consent. Put a stop to this. Put whoever is so free with your time and energy on notice never to lend you out without first asking. And if they already have, feel no compunction about begging off on the grounds you have prior commitments that weren't considered at the time. Why make yourself crazy?

143
Gird yourself for ineptitude on the road.

Today, it's not *if* another motorist will do something stupid every time you're out driving...but *when.* So be ready for it. Drive calmly yet alertly so you can quickly react to any surprises they'll spring on you. Expect that the car ahead will cut in front of you without signaling...that another vehicle will always be glued to your rear bumper...that an oncoming car won't dim its high beams until it's crested a hill and blinded you. Expect it, drive defensively in anticipation of it, and you'll enjoy a smoother, less stressful ride. (And you'll be less likely to do something stupid yourself.) Why make yourself crazy?

144
Don't be sucked in by euphemistic language.

People have ways of coloring things more rosily than they really are. So when you hear them say things like the following (in quotes), be alert to what they *really* mean (in parentheses): "I shouldn't be long." (Hope you brought a book with you.) "Our prices are competitive." (We're just as expensive as everyone else.) "Some assembly required." (What are you doing this weekend?) "We can still be friends." (There will be a brief interim period before I dump you altogether.) "You have been specially selected to participate in this once-in-a-lifetime offer." (We got your name off a certified chump list.) "There's a 50% chance of rain." (Your guess is as good as ours.) "We'll have to get together for lunch sometime." (Have a nice life.) When you hear any of the above, or similar statements, don't take it too seriously. Why make yourself crazy?

145
Hang out with calm people.

Granted, it's not easy to find them today. But when you do, don't let them get away...their reflected equanimity will soothe your soul. Just as hanging out with stressed people will leave you utterly hyper. Stress is contagious. So it's imperative you periodically remove yourself from your wired cohorts...and seek the calming companionship of those content just to let life happen. Observe how good a life that can be. Then take a hard look at what you're racing toward. Why make yourself crazy?

146
Improve your posture.

Try not to slouch. Because when you slouch—for example, slunk low in your office chair, hunched over while walking, or ensconced deeply in the cushions of your couch—it impedes the flow of blood, makes breathing more difficult, contributes to a feeling of stressful incapacity that makes it harder to hoist yourself to a task. Snap to it. Sit up straight. Profit from the energy and alertness of a good healthy posture. Why make yourself crazy?

147
Learn from your ill-fated
past purchases.

Consider all the little-used merchandise (junk?) you purchased over the years...the seemed-like-a-good-idea-at-the-time stuff that's now needlessly clogging your home. Like that yogurt maker up in the attic. The ear-splitting electric broom. That ridiculous exercise contraption. The cappuccino machine. Things you probably couldn't unload in a tag sale. Get rid of them. But first, spend a moment with each to ponder the stress you endured to earn the money for it, shop for it, store it, and subsequently squirm over the folly of it. Then take that intelligence and apply it the next time you get an urge to buy something of suspect value. Avoid the hassle, save the money, experience the liberating feeling of doing without. Why make yourself crazy?

148
Cancel that last chore of the night.

When you can barely stay awake...are losing your focus...getting more and more frustrated...making stupid mistakes...call it a day. Even better, don't wait till you get to that stage. Knock off while you're still alert, still optimistic, still have a little gas left to wind down peacefully. (Like leaving the table a little hungry.) Don't let that last task do you in. End each day on a positive note that will carry you into the next. Why make yourself crazy?

149
Don't let stress make you an ogre.

What stress can do to us isn't pretty. Snapping at others. Becoming impatient, insensitive, quick to criticize and berate. Often hurtful to those we love. Even boiling over into tirades and tantrums. In the name of what? If this is what your quest for the "good life" is doing to you, maybe it's not such a good life after all. Think about the inordinate pressure you're putting on yourself. Day after day. Year after year. It's taking a toll. Compromising your health. Giving you gray hairs. Turning you into someone you're not. Life can be carefree and fun now if you let it. Lighten up. Lose the stress. Why make yourself crazy?

150
Be careful what you say in the heat of the moment.

Statements made in a fit of anger, passion, fear, elation, frustration, or bravado can often dig you into a hole agonizingly difficult to climb out of. How many needless stressful situations we blurt ourselves into! Train yourself in intense moments to hold your tongue until you're able to think rationally...and prevent yourself from making promises, claims, accusations, or commitments you'll later regret. When the emotional level rises and you're tempted to say something momentous...zip it. Why make yourself crazy?

151
Learn to live with daily "stresslets."

"Stresslets" are those momentary little delays, disruptions or setbacks that cause a pin prick of aggravation dozens, even hundreds of times a day. Examples: a webpage taking an extra second to load, a jarring phone interruption, an untied shoelace, a misplaced pen, a dropped file folder. Stresslets are a product of our high-tech, fast-paced expectations...a growing intolerance to glitches of any kind. They can shorten your breath, heighten tension, promote irritability... and lumped together, add up to major stress. You simply have to factor them in as a given in life, roll with them and weigh their insignificance against the enormous gains in productivity and convenience you enjoy today. Don't get strung out over stresslets. Why make yourself crazy?

152
Lose that jarring morning alarm.

If your alarm clock shocks you out of bed each day with a sudden, loud, jangling noise, you could be doing yourself harm—starting the day with a burst of unwanted stress hormones. Try one of those new wake-up clocks that lift you gently out of sleep with natural sounds like ocean surf, birds, rainfall, or babbling brooks. Some even have pleasant chime sequences that gradually increase in volume. Or wake up to an unobtrusive radio station. Set a melodious rather than dissonant note for the day. Why make yourself crazy?

153
If you don't like something, change it.

There is no "they." Only you and I. So next time you grumble that "they" should do this, or "they" should do that...what you're really saying is someone other than you should do it. Or essentially nobody. If you want change, *you* have to effect it. Or at least contribute to it. By taking action, writing letters or voting a certain way. If you think it's fruitless, consider that every change ever made usually had someone behind it. So you can either go on living life the way others want you to. Or you can change things. And the sooner you get started, the sooner you can stop stressing about it. Why make yourself crazy?

154
Don't talk so fast.

Have you noticed how much faster the pace of normal conversation is becoming? How we rush our words, leaving no openings, anxious to complete a thought before someone else rushes in? Often having to scold our listeners with "let me finish"? It's a sign of our hurried times. And as much as fast talking is driven by stress, it can cause stress, too. Rapid speech is highly contagious. It's less effective, hard to follow and easily misconstrued. No matter how fast the other guy is blathering on, slow down, speak deliberately... replace speed with firmness and clarity. You'll stay more calm and communicate more forcefully. Why make yourself crazy?

155
Don't stress over what to say.

We often reproach ourselves for not finding the right words at the right time. We deplore awkward pauses and fumbled utterances. We get frustrated that we're not as coherent, quick-witted, eloquent and incisive as people on TV or in the movies. Hey, you'd be pretty glib, too, if you had professional writers putting words into your mouth. But that isn't reality. Life is full of clumsy dialog. You can't articulate eloquently every moment of the day. So accept it and move on. Why make yourself crazy?

156
Don't let your backlog of projects get you down.

There are things you need to take care of that aren't getting done. And it's eating away at you, because it's not like you to let things go like that. But your overloaded schedule isn't yielding an inch right now. The thing *not* to do is torture yourself about it.

You're not a shirker, you're not irresponsible if you flat out can't get to it. So ease up on yourself. If you have every intention of completing these projects, you will. As unlikely as it seems now, the time will present itself. And true to your ethic, you'll come through. Why make yourself crazy?

157
Be a team player.

It's more productive—and less stressful—to work as a team. In your job, in your family, in your community. When you spread the work and responsibility around the pressure eases, everyone becomes more cooperative. As much as we like to think of ourselves as complete packages, we're not. We need others to contribute what we lack, to balance out our collective strengths and weaknesses. Let go the urge to put it all on yourself or take all the credit. Society is a team effort and success most gratifying when everyone's involved. Why make yourself crazy?

158
Get three estimates for every major project.

Regardless how wonderful you think the first outfit is, always get a second and third proposal for any important household or business project. It will introduce you to perspectives you hadn't even considered. And establish a sound basis for comparison. You'll be surprised at how differently the same job can be approached. And what you'll learn in the winnowing process. Go for the proverbial three estimates and be three times wiser, have three times the negotiating leverage and be three times less likely to make a bad choice. Why make yourself crazy?

159
Don't be a gossip.
(Or an eager listener of it.)

Running down others isn't the way to boost your own esteem. On the contrary, it can foster feelings of self-disgust, betrayal and guilt—or the perverse wish that your revelations will prove true. Talking ill of others makes it harder to ever view those people in a fair light or change your opinion of them. And it may leave your listeners wary you'll spread stories about them, too. Gossip may seem a quick and easy way to vent, or provide juicy entertainment, but it comes at a steep price. Better to mind your own business. Why make yourself crazy?

160
Have at least one meal
a day as a family.

How long do you think a company would survive if its workers rarely met to find out what everyone else was doing? Yet many families, with so much at stake, often go days without even sharing a meal. Mealtime is more than a social event. It's a vital means of communication—a time to make plans, vent concerns, express feelings, work out differences, and most of all show that you love, support and care for each other. The family meal is a bedrock of family stability...and shouldn't fall victim to busy schedules. Take care of things on the home front first. Insist on a daily family repast and work out schedules to make it happen. Not easy, but absolutely worth it. Why make yourself crazy?

161
Dance.

Few activities deliver as many benefits. Yet too few people ever get to enjoy them. Dancing is fun. An easy way to make friends. Great exercise. And an excellent way to release tension and stress. There are dances for every taste and ability—from ballroom to break, swing to free-form. Take lessons and become a skilled dancer. Or just get silly dancing with the kids, friends or yourself in front of a mirror. Why wait for that infrequent wedding or social event to reap the pleasures of dancing? Plan an evening of dancing out. Or stay in. Just roll up the rug, kick up your heels and start moving to the music. Why make yourself crazy?

162
Stop beating up on yourself.

Just the fact that you're overscheduled, rushing around and stressed out should send you the message you're doing your best. Even going beyond the call. It's not you that's the problem, it's your out-of-control lifestyle. Getting down on yourself will only make you feel worse. (How demoralizing to knock yourself out all day and still feel like you're behind!) Instead, eliminate needless activities driven by fear, outside pressure and insecurity...and concentrate on what's truly important to you and your family. Your self-esteem can't help but soar. Why make yourself crazy?

163
Give your house a breath of fresh air.

Houses today are so well insulated and airtight, they're just as effective at keeping fresh air out as they are the heat and cold. Thus, germs are allowed

to breed and thrive, cooking fumes and other con-
taminants remain trapped inside—especially in winter—promoting colds, flu, asthma, and other respira-
tory ailments. Not to mention the odorous build-up of
stale air that leaves us ornery, stressed and dull-
witted. Keeping a window cracked on each side of the
house, or the upper and lower extremities, will help to
circulate clean, fresh air. And once a day, if only for a
short while, open wide several windows to create a
wholesale exchange of air. It'll leave you much more
perky, healthy and alert. Why make yourself crazy?

164
See the humor in things.

Life can be very funny. But if you're constantly
stressed out or harried, you can miss much of the fun
going on around you. Why deny yourself this delightful
and rejuvenating aspect of life? Try to remain in good
spirits, even when confronted by aggravating circumstances. Laugh at your mistakes and encourage others
to laugh at theirs, too. Humor is contagious, and a
readiness to laugh an endearing and beneficial quality.
A little laughter can go a long way toward lightening up
a business meeting, easing a tense relationship or getting you through a trying time. Enjoy a good chuckle
every so often. Why make yourself crazy?

165
Lose an argument.

That's right, lose an argument. When was the last time you looked someone squarely in the face and said, "You know, you're right. I'm wrong. Thanks for straightening me out." Hard to do, isn't it? We'd sooner cling to a worthless position than admit we're in error. But a humbling concession now and then is a great relief. Because it removes the onerous pressure of trying to defend a flawless façade. An image that fools no one. And displays weakness rather than character. (Don't we see it every day in our politicians?) Lose an argument. Show humility. You'll gain a lot more respect and credibility. Why make yourself crazy?

166
Eat a healthy breakfast.

Loading up on caffeine and sugar (coffee and donuts) is like burning poor quality fuel: you have to keep pumping more in or you'll fizzle out altogether. And leave yourself jittery, tense and irritable. Skipping breakfast is even worse. Why start your day at a distinct disadvantage? Eat a solid breakfast. For example, a high-protein cereal (like old-fashioned oatmeal), fresh fruit and skim milk. It'll dish out a steady flow of energy for hours. Forget the sticky buns. Start the day at peak performance by putting some quality gas in your tank. Why make yourself crazy?

167
Call an old friend.

Out of the blue. Someone you knew before you built up those barriers of wariness and guardedness that keep more current friends at arm's length. Someone you can drop all pretense with, be comfortable with, just be yourself with, who will help melt away those tensions and pressures that now beset you. No matter how long you've been out of touch with an old friend, you can pick up where you left off as if no time has elapsed. Reconnect with someone from your more halcyon, carefree days. It'll do you a world of good. Why make yourself crazy?

168
Avoid the stress of monotony.

Does your life taste like reheated leftovers? If the fun and excitement seem to have gone, don't fret about it. It doesn't mean you've exhausted all experience and there's nothing left to get excited about. Far from it. You've merely plateaued. Or dug yourself into a rut. The solution is simply to climb up to another level, to strike out in new directions. It'll take some effort, not to mention risk, but the rewards can be phenomenal. So be bold, be daring. Life is full of endless surprises just waiting for you to discover. Why make yourself crazy?

169
Eliminate stress-induced writer's block.

Whether it's a business memo, presentation, report, article, or even an important email...when you're under stress the words don't flow. The thought process jams, the creative juices dry up. Here's what to do. Take a deep breath, relax and clear your mind. Then get something down. Anything. If you can't find the right words, just get the thoughts out no matter how crude they sound. (Like an artist doing a rough sketch.) Now at least you have something to work with, to edit, to improve—and the stress will begin to ease. Each time you revisit the piece, you'll find a way to refine, reorganize and add to it, and you'll soon have the project in hand. Why make yourself crazy?

170
Start your holiday shopping *early*.

You'll be able to do it in a more leisurely, composed manner. Stores will be less crowded. Selections will be at their fullest. Pre-holiday sales will save you money. And sales clerks may even be pleasant. Put it off and you risk that last-minute craziness you swore you'd never put yourself through again. Overcrowded stores, traffic jams, and mile-away parking. Frantic searches for hot toys already sold out. Agonizingly long checkout lines. And dealing with overwhelmed, under-trained Christmas help. Who needs it, on top of all your other stress? Even if you're not yet in a holiday mood...fake it. Start shopping, get it done. And enjoy the holiday season. Why make yourself crazy?

171
Don't let unhealthy job
stress persist.

If your workload or project is impossible to complete without pulling your hair out, doing a slapdash job or suffering a near stroke for your trouble, speak up early on rather than bottle it up and be unable to perform the work accurately and professionally. And do it in a positive way, without complaining, by offering possible solutions: you'll need more time; you can do *part* of the project in the allotted time; or you'll require more help. If you're a good competent worker your request should command respect and compliance. It doesn't help anyone to say nothing and let it eat away at your well-being, and subject both you and your company to poor performance. Why make yourself crazy?

172
Don't become addicted to your work.

Be aware of signs that your job has become your master rather than the other way around. For instance, you work at night and on weekends, even when you don't really have to. Or you find yourself putting family members and other activities off in favor of getting a few more work-related things out of the way. Or you're constantly thinking about your job, even at the most, uh, inappropriate of times. Embrace the philosophy that you don't live to work, you work too live. And remember, all that superfluous time spent on the job...is time you'll never see again. Why make yourself crazy?

173
Don't let stress play havoc with your memory.

And well it might. When you're constantly stressed, you can't remember much of anything. You forget the simplest things, like names, places and phone numbers (even your own!). Think how impossible it is to find something when you're rushing out the door. Or recall a computer procedure when you're under the gun. Here's a temporary fix. Take a deep breath and relax to un-clutter your mind. Even take your mind off it for a few seconds (like not looking directly at an object to see it better in the dark). It'll come to you. But that's not the answer. Losing the stress is. If you want to improve your memory...simply remember to keep applying these stress-reducing strategies. Why make yourself crazy?

174
Don't pay for everything twice.

Once with your money and again with your resentment. Getting angry every time you reach for your wallet is high blood pressure hell. Things cost. And invariably they cost more than we expect them to. Still more every time prices go up—and you can bet they will. It's a fact of life you have to accept. Letting it eat away at you only does unnecessary harm. Replace those ill feelings with positive ones. Like what you're getting, not what you're spending. And if you really don't think it's worth the tab, shop around for a better deal. Or do without. Why make yourself crazy?

175
Ease up. You don't have to be perfect.

You can strive to be, but don't be bummed out if you're not. No one is. Being obsessed with perfection is a source of unrelenting stress. And falling short of it, which is inevitable, certain disappointment. A fine thank you for great effort expended! You should be feeling good about what you accomplish...and not dwell on minor flaws. Learn to accept less than perfect and take your satisfaction in always having given it your best. Why make yourself crazy?

176
Observe other people under stress.

Notice how they rush things. How tense and wound up they can get. How they're always apologizing for falling behind or making mistakes. How they never seem to be in control, bouncing from one thing to the next, leaving loose ends and unfinished business in their wake. That may be YOU! Or where you're headed. So study people under stress and think about how they could improve their lives. (We're always better at critiquing others, aren't we?) Then apply that counsel to your own life. You can learn a lot about yourself simply by observing others. Why make yourself crazy?

177
Observe yourself.

Go through a day as if you were an objective observer following yourself around, monitoring your every
thought, emotion and action. Note with honesty what
annoys you, or makes you pleased, angry, tense, proud,
or frustrated. Observe how you act in certain situations...and why. You'll learn a lot. (And not always like
what you'll learn.) But the experience will be eye-
opening. And allow you to identify what's stressing you
most—things you may not even be aware of! Which you
can then fix. Try to see yourself as objectively as other
people do. Why make yourself crazy?

178
Chip away at projects with
long lead times.

When you get an assignment with a "luxury" of
time, don't squander it. Get at least a start on it right
away, when your enthusiasm and understanding of it
are at a peak. Then spend a little time on it each day
to keep the momentum going. That way, every
thought you have of the project will be a positive one:
"I'm on the case, I'm getting it done." Put it off, and
every thought will be increasingly negative: "Yikes, I
haven't even started yet!" Which can add up to big

stress over time. And a major crisis as the deadline nears, you've forgotten what to do, and your enthusiasm has been supplanted by anxiety and dread. Get it going early. You'll do a better job, in less time, without the stress. Why make yourself crazy?

179
Take care of minor nuisances right away.

Do you get so rushed and crazed you won't even pause to correct a pesky annoyance? Like a shirt label scratching your neck; a mouse cord that's too short; a pebble in your shoe; a stack of folders annoyingly in the way; glaring sunlight stealing through the window? Take care of these gremlins as soon as they present themselves. Because the longer you let them go, the bigger the monster they grow into...to the point where they become totally exasperating. Stop these small, relentless tortures in their tracks. Why make yourself crazy?

180
Learn how to swim upstream.

Not easy when everyone else is rushing along in the opposite direction, caught up in the daily frenzy of impossible schedules, frantic deadlines and excessive activities. But if you're truly determined to rid your life of stress for good, you have to fight the current, learn how to say no and cut back on your involvements. It's a constant battle, and some people aren't going to like it, but it's your life, your well-being, your peace of mind at stake. Resist being swept along in directions you don't want to go. Why make yourself crazy?

181
Don't let timesaving devices *steal* your time.

Many do. For example, that kitchen gadget with all the attachments that slices, dices, chops, shreds, etc.? Make sure it doesn't take longer to retrieve, set up, use, take apart, clean up, and put away than simply doing it by hand. (If you can figure where you stored the thing in the first place.) Also, any appliance you use so infrequently you have to reread a complicated set of instructions each time...may not be worth the trouble. In essence, be suspect of any "miracle time-saver" with a lot of parts to assemble (especially plastic, which inevitably breaks), takes up a lot of space, is a headache to clean, and has a steep, easily forgotten learning curve. They'll not only hog your time...they spell S-T-R-E-S-S. Why make yourself crazy?

182
Study in shorter, more
frequent intervals.

Whether it's schoolwork or a career training program...overnight cramming and marathon study sessions are less productive and the material more easily
forgotten. Never let it get to that point. Study as you
go along—in shorter, more frequent intervals. It will
keep the information fresh in your mind so you won't
waste time relearning it. Review sessions will be
faster and less onerous—thus, less likely to be put
off. And you'll be assured of understanding the material long after the final exam. Which is entirely the
point, isn't it? Study as you go. You'll study less...and
retain more. Why make yourself crazy?

183
Take a tech holiday.

Spend a day unplugged. No cell phones, TVs, computers, video games, DVDs, personal stereos, (and this
is tough) PDAs, or other digitally fed distractions. Instead, strive to have face-to-face conversations, read
books, take walks, play with the kids, visit friends, or
just sit quietly and think. Find out how soothing and
restorative it is to be UNconnected once in a while. And
how refreshing it is to take a break from our growing

dependency on these devices, which are meant to be tools, not ends in themselves. Keep technology in its proper perspective. And your humanity first and foremost. Why make yourself crazy?

184
If you think stress, you'll live stress.

As if you don't already have enough real stress to deal with, you're always thinking about it, too. Which makes your life even more stressful. Try not to give thought to past, present or future crazed days, pressure situations, mortifying blunders, or charged events. It will only make you experience their intensity again and again—increasing your anxiety and spiking your blood pressure—without even having done anything! Banish these destructive thoughts, and only allow calm, soothing ones to enter your emotional domain. It will spare you an enormous amount of anxiety over time. Why make yourself crazy?

185
Work at being patient.

Patience is not something you have, it is something you *do*. It is a disservice to say of someone "I wish I had her patience," as if it was merely a possession that doesn't require much effort. Patience is work, difficult work. But for those who strive for it, the rewards are many: smoother relationships, fewer conflicts, less stress, and an ability to stick it out long enough to gain a deeper understanding and enjoyment of life. Next time you lament "I have no patience for that," realize that you *could* have the patience, and all its attendant benefits, if you simply worked at it. Why make yourself crazy?

186
Delegate.

Stress is often caused by an inability to let go, a constant need to micromanage, the fear that everything will fall apart the minute you turn your back. It leaves you hung up on time-consuming details, stifles the participation and growth of others, and creates unnecessary tension all around. Take the leap of faith. Learn to delegate. Assign responsibilities and give others the chance to prove themselves. You can dole it out gradually, to gain confidence and minimize error, but begin unburdening yourself of the oppressive minutia that's needlessly choking your life. You can experience a marked reduction in stress in a relatively short period of time simply by delegating. Why make yourself crazy?

187
Know when to terminate
an encounter.

In our politeness or reluctance to offend another, we often let visits, dates, conversations, or meetings drag on far longer than they need to—creating stale, stressful, awkward situations. Take charge at such times. When things show signs of winding down naturally, use the opportunity to break in and wrap it up, before it grows tedious. You're not being rude, you're being considerate of both of you. Think how you aren't put out when another person has to leave; indeed, you would feel bad holding them up. Terminate your encounters while they're still fresh, and you'll save something for next time, too. Why make yourself crazy?

188
Don't groom your kids
for a life of stress.

In your efforts to expose your child to every known activity, sport and pursuit on the planet, you may be guaranteeing them one thing. A stressed-out future. Regardless of what you tell them, rushing frantically from venue to venue sends the message that this is the way life proceeds. They'll inevitably follow suit.

Start setting a different example now. Pare down activities so each one can be more richly and leisurely enjoyed. Build in more free, unpressured time that lets their imaginations take flight. Kids are notoriously overscheduled. And they hardly need to experience everything before adulthood, or what will be left? Removing that stress from their life—and yours— will leave everyone healthier and happier. Why make yourselves crazy?

189
Give a gift when there's no reason to.

Yes, it's fun to give gifts on birthdays, holidays and anniversaries. But isn't it more or less required, or at least expected? And aren't we celebrating the event more than the person? Give a gift to someone when it's *not* expected. See how really good it will make the both of you feel. The best part is, gifts of this nature can be small and inexpensive and still have a wonderful effect. Because it's a genuine expression of friendship, love or appreciation. And shifts the focus back to who—rather than what—is important in life. Stop off and pick up a surprise gift. Why make yourself crazy?

190
Reject rejection.

You were turned down for a job. You were refused a date. Your ideas were dismissed in a meeting. You didn't make the team. Your proposal was shot down. Your loan wasn't approved. Yes, it hurts. And the best way to deal with it—rather than sulk, despair or give up altogether—is to do something immediately to counter it. Apply somewhere else. Revise your proposal. Try a new tactic. Choose a different prospect. Change your approach. Or simply make yourself irresistible. Anything to take the emphasis off the negative and reestablish some optimism—relegating rejection to its rightful place: a mere bump along the way. Why make yourself crazy?

191
Fire yourself.

If you're constantly running late, overscheduling your days, making far too many mistakes, rushing around in a dither, doing everything in a slapdash manner...fire yourself! Because what you're doing now simply isn't working. So start over. Rethink things. And hire a new, different you to manage your life. One who doesn't say yes to anything until you've weighed its demands against your time and energy.

One who realizes it's actually more productive (and infinitely more rewarding) to do fewer things well than many things badly. Like a company that sells off a poorly performing subsidiary, rid your life of needless pursuits that do little more than compound the chaos. If your current lifestyle isn't cutting it, give it the pink slip. Why make yourself crazy?

192
Beware the stress of envy.

How much envy burns inside you daily? How much resentment do you feel when you compare what you have with others and come up short? This can be a constant source of stress...and simmering anger. It shifts the focus away from what's good in your life to what you lack. All of us to some degree envy those who achieve remarkable success in their careers, relationships, investments, athletic endeavors, and other pursuits. It's a natural response. But when we allow it to persist, it eats away at our happiness and self-esteem. If anything, the accomplishments of others should inspire and motivate you, not drag you down. Accept that life doesn't dole out talent, intelligence, circumstances, or luck very evenly. So measure yourself not against what others have achieved, but the efforts you've made to develop the abilities you've been given. Why make yourself crazy?

193
Beware the stress of euphoria.

When something wonderful has happened to you, or you're anticipating an exciting upcoming event or recognition, you're naturally going to be elated, walking on air. But dwelling on it excessively can leave you *too* wired, causing you to get overly distracted, lose sleep, become irritable, and be an irritation to others. This kind of stress is insidious, because it creeps up on you when you're least expecting it, when things are going well. Take a deep breath, relax, get busy on other things, and draw out the enjoyment of your good fortune over time. Because the positives can wear on your nerves almost as much as the negatives. Why make yourself crazy?

194
Entertaining is supposed to be fun, remember?

When you throw a dinner party or host a get-together, it's not an audition, you're not on trial and your guests aren't judges and juries. Yet that's how you might see it—something to fret about, even dread.

Which, if you're worried things won't go well, will all but assure it. Remember, it's not about you. It's about inviting people into your home and making them feel welcome and comfortable. If you're tense and unsure, that's what they'll pick up on. (How many times have you attended a tautly wound event and had a perfectly lousy time?) So make it fun. Be casual, gracious, spontaneous. You'll be a hit, and so will your party. Why make yourself crazy?

195
Write down infrequently used procedures.

There are some things you do at intervals just far enough apart you forget how you did them last time. Which is terribly frustrating, having to learn them all over again. And again. For example, how you strung up the Christmas lights...drove to a particular destination...reset the clock on your answering machine... changed your wiper blades. As much as you think you'll remember these routines next time, you won't. So take a brief moment and write them in a notebook or PDA while they're fresh in your mind. And keep it handy. You won't be kicking yourself every time something needs redoing. Why make yourself crazy?

196
Rotate working on different projects.

For example, if you have three projects due next week, performing them in their entirety one after the other can make each seem long, drawn out and tiresome. Instead, divide your time each day into thirds and work on all three. Each project will provide a refreshing break from the others, while allowing you to make steady progress on all. Like a farmer rotating crops to keep the soil rich and fertile, varying tasks will keep you more alert and imaginative, making the work proceed more quickly and enjoyably. Why make yourself crazy?

197
Don't be a victim of the
rebate runaround.

What looks like an irresistible sale price is often enfeebled by the sneaky little cop-out "after rebate." When you see those words you should consider running the other way. It means if you want a discount you'll have to work for it. Filling out forms, making photocopies and mailing what amounts to a dossier. Then you'll wait for it. And wait for it. Why be a stooge for manufacturers and retailers who are all the while earning interest on *your* money...worse, hoping you'll forget to apply for your rebate, or making the process so irksome you'll simply give up. How cheesy. Do business with companies who'll give you a good honest discount up front, rather than make you jump through hoops to get it. Why make yourself crazy?

198
Buy a car for its safety and dependability first.

Today's automobile ads are like car chase scenes from action-adventure flicks. Fast, unsafe driving is glamorously—and irresponsibly—promoted. (Aren't they concerned that thousands of people, especially young people, die each year in speeding accidents?) Another ploy is to showcase a vehicle's alluring curves. Still another, the status of its expensive nameplate. All intended to appeal to your emotional rather than practical sense. If getting places safely for many years to come is your primary reason for buying a car in the first place, don't fall for these diversionary tactics. Get good, hard, objective research on a vehicle's safety and reliability. You'll save yourself untold stress, trouble and disappointment. Ask yourself this. When the novelty of owning a sexy car wears off, which will happen all too soon, what will you be left with? Why make yourself crazy?

199
Take care of your people problems first.

It's tempting to seek refuge in your work or busy schedule, rather than confront more ticklish human issues (like smoothing over a strained relationship with a family member or associate). But trying to ignore the problem won't cut it. That nagging uneasiness will shadow you everywhere, distract and distress you until you tackle it head on. Settling your differences with others, reaching an understanding, freeing your mind of interpersonal baggage should be your top priority. People problems first. Why make yourself crazy?

200
Readily give out and receive hugs.

Studies have shown that hugs can reduce stress and tension appreciably. Obviously, some of us aren't overt huggers and may shy away from such a suggestion. (And granted, it may be more stressful to hug someone you dislike.) But if you can get past the initial awkwardness, you'll find a good deal of relief in the occasional squeeze. Your spouse, children, parents, and other loved ones are all good candidates for hugs. Even a quick embrace between friends as part of a greeting eases tension. The best thing is, two people can benefit from one hug! That's a pretty efficient way to reduce stress. So hug early and hug often. Why make yourself crazy?

201
Listen to music that will soothe your soul.

For each of us, there's a musical genre or composition that has the ability to dispel our stress and anxiety. You just have to know what it is. For some, soft and soothing works well. For others, loud and rhythmic. If you aren't sure, sample some selections at a music store and pick up CDs or downloads that do the trick for you. Then, when things start to go haywire, pull out your personal stereo and let the tunes lull you back to an even keel. Many people already avail themselves of this surefire stress reducer. You should, too. Why make yourself crazy?

202
Be honest.

Live with integrity and you'll deal with a lot less stress in your life. Because dishonesty, deception, cheating—aside from their obvious moral implications— require constant, nerve-wracking upkeep...covering your tracks, deluding others, living with the specter of getting caught. However small our dishonesties (and who among us is guiltless?), they will exact a costly toll in undermining our sense of security, well-being and self-respect. Which may explain why some of the most honest people in the world—regardless of their financial circumstances—are also the happiest. When we come clean, and live clean, a huge burden is lifted. Why make yourself crazy?

203
Release your stress through creative expression.

Put your imagination to work. Be creative. Dream. Stepping beyond the boundaries of narrowed perspectives will set your mind free, expand your possibilities, excite and energize you. "But I'm not the creative type," you say. Perhaps not in the way we generally view creativity: art, music, writing. But each of us is creative in our own way. Maybe it's building something, organizing a community group, undertaking a new athletic endeavor, planning a unique social event. You have talents (and you know this) that aren't being fully utilized because of your all-consuming, over-stressed lifestyle. Break out of it. Get busy. And create. Why make yourself crazy?

204
Read the instructions in full first.

There's a reason why they tell you to read a product's instruction manual in its entirety before operating it. Too many people think they can figure it out on their own. Or they're pressed for time and just wing it. So very often they assemble it wrong, can't get it to work properly, operate it unsafely, or break it altogether. They become totally exasperated with the product, and disgusted with themselves. All of this can be avoided by taking the time to sit down, relax, read the instructions, and familiarize yourself with the item first. In the long run, you'll spare yourself much aggravation and enjoy its benefits to the fullest. Why make yourself crazy?

205
Seek professional help for
major stress problems.

The stress we deal with in this book is the everyday stress, the retail stress that we more or less bring on ourselves and thus have the power to eliminate ourselves. But sometimes there are major stressful events in our lives we don't have control over—an illness, death of a loved one, marriage breakup, loss of a job, depression, abusive relationship—that require the help of a professional therapist. In such cases, don't put off seeking assistance, or believe that casual stress remedies are going to do the trick. There are people out there who can make an extraordinary difference in helping you get through a difficult time. Seek their counsel. Why make yourself crazy?

206
Be an advocate for stress-free living.

You probably already are, if you're making headway with these tips. Because the changes you've made are almost certainly being noticed...and setting an example. Beyond that, you can take a proactive role in promoting a less stressful environment wherever you are. Allude to others how richer your life is becoming without the constant pressure, rushing and overscheduling. And without being preachy, suggest they try some of these strategies, too. When you do that, you're further reducing the stress in your own life because fewer people will be making *you* crazy. And they in turn will help to de-stress other people...and so on. Think of the chain reaction you could start, and all the good you can accomplish, by advocating a stress-free lifestyle. Why make yourself crazy?

A good place to start is to share this book with someone you know who sorely needs it!

207
Celebrate your feet.

Yes, your feet. You take them way too much for granted. Spend a day and honor them. Care for them. Because feet are amazing. They get you where you want to go. Frequently do overtime. Take a lot of abuse. Yet rarely complain. (Except for an occasional blistering protest.) So today, give something back. Treat them to a massage. Stretch them out. Clean them up. Clip the nails. Maybe even splurge on a pedicure, a comfortable new pair of shoes, or soft slippers. Think how vital your feet are. How skillfully they hold you up, shuttle you around and perform countless incredible...well... feats. From this day on, appreciate the wonderful gifts that are your feet...and all the possibilities they bring to your life. Why make yourself crazy?

208
Don't live your life through a camera lens.

Sometimes we're so anxious to get our trip, milestone or special occasion on film, we all but miss the event itself! Look, you're never going to enjoy something more than when it's actually happening. So why blunt the experience by peering at it through a viewfinder? Or fussing over angles, poses and camera settings? A couple of quick snapshots or video clips will suffice to chronicle the event and establish the who, what, when, and where. Most of these pictures usually end up in a shoebox anyway, rarely if ever seen. Be a participant rather than an observer. Your first-hand memory will be far more poignant than anything you put on a disk. Why make yourself crazy?

209
Eliminate excessive and superfluous activities.

Today, we run up time debt faster than we do credit card debt. And it's a debt we can't repay. It happens when we plan, sign up and agree to do things without considering how long they'll take or where we'll fit them into our schedule. And that's inviting conflicts, chaos, mad dashes, late arrivals, no-shows, bruised feelings, and disappointing experiences. If this is life in the fast lane, maybe you should change lanes. Time is precious. Be selective how you dole yours out. Limit your pursuits to what you can fully and leisurely enjoy. Remember, every activity must be prepared for, gotten to, participated in, and returned from. Don't overbook yourself like the airlines do. You're just asking for trouble. Why make yourself crazy?

210
Always have a list when
you go food shopping.

Trying to plan menus in the store, or recall what you need from memory—amid thousands of available items—can soon become exasperating. A waster of time in an effort to save it. Even if you need just a few items, jot them down since inevitably you'll forget one. And check the kitchen first so you don't spend time and money buying what you already have. Categorize your list, too, according to the store's layout. Today's supermarkets are so huge, if you miss something you have to walk half a mile to go back for it. A little forethought, and a simple list, can make food shopping a lot more palatable. Why make yourself crazy?

211
Protest with your pocketbook.

Sadly, it seems the only way to get people to do the right thing these days is to put the squeeze on them financially. It's the one thing that's certain to get their attention. So don't buy the products of companies, do business with merchants or contribute to "non-profits" whose policies, practices or advertising you find questionable. No, you won't bring a big outfit to its knees. But you'll enjoy the satisfaction of knowing they're not getting your money. And perhaps the money of others you pass along your concerns to. Also, make your disapproval known to the culprits. Call toll-free customer service lines when available and voice your complaints on their dime. Do nothing and the issue will continue to rankle you. Exercise the power you have, however small, and hit them where it hurts most. In the wallet. Why make yourself crazy?

212
Don't always feel you have to reciprocate.

Are you the type of person who thanks people for their thank-you notes? Feels unworthy when you receive a gift? Or indebted because you enjoyed another's hospitality? Enough already. Learn how to accept the generosity of others without laying a guilt trip on yourself. Or feeling you have to reciprocate immediately. After all, that would diminish what's been done for you, wouldn't it? And it probably wasn't the intention of the giver to make you feel beholden, was it? Just as you wouldn't want your recipients to feel you're expecting a quick payback. So next time someone does something nice for you, don't fret about it. Simply enjoy it! Why make yourself crazy?

213
Dress down.

Whenever you're "off-duty," or the formalities are over, or you no longer need to impress...ease into looser, more comfortably fitting clothes. (The kind you'd wear wrestling on the floor with the kids.) You'll shed a good deal of stress along with the tighter-fitting, more formal apparel. In fact, choosing casual as your default style instead of costly and confining clothes is cheaper, safer (you're less a target for would-be muggers) and you'll feel really special on those occasions when you do dress up. Take a tip from today's teens (at least the guys) and chill out in laid-back, loose attire. Why make yourself crazy?

214
Always keep pictures of
loved ones around.

In your home. In your office. In your wallet. You can't have too many reminders of who and what make it all worthwhile...to bring you back to the important things...to relegate current trials to their proper place in the broader scheme. Pictures of children, parents, grandparents, and other loved ones—present and past—instantly conjure up feelings of warmth and affection. Look up occasionally from your desk, kitchen counter or work area and let those images soothe and reassure you. Why make yourself crazy?

215
Eat fresh.

There's something to be said for eating fresh, un-processed, natural foods. After all, these are what got us here in the first place, aren't they? Beyond the nutritional benefits, it's therapeutic to stop off at local food markets each day and pick up fresh fish, meats, breads, fruits and vegetables...as opposed to frozen, processed, canned, or heaven-knows-what. Perhaps we're satisfying some primal hunter-gatherer urge, in the most literal way, to provide for ourselves and our family. Whatever's at play, it has a way of easing our stress, soothing us with the reassuring feeling that we're fulfilling a basic need. Go out and shop for the makings of a good fresh meal tonight. It's time well spent. Why make yourself crazy?

216
Don't become addicted to
instant gratification.

Everybody today wants results. Now. And woe to those who can't deliver. As if it's our birthright to get all that we want immediately. We abhor waiting for anything: traffic lights, meals, store checkouts, re-pairpersons, winning teams, babies, success...even five seconds of dead TV air ticks us off. As fast as things are done for us, we demand even faster. And when it doesn't happen, which is often, we become indignant, exasperated, stressed out. *Let it go.* Break this unquenchable need for instant results or you'll never be satisfied with anything. Let life unfold natu-rally. Its best and most enduring joys don't happen in a flash...but in their own good time. Why make yourself crazy?

217
Don't assume others learn from their mistakes.

You've been the unlucky victim of another's error. But just because they acknowledge and apologize for it (often merely lip service) doesn't mean they won't do it again. In fact, it's more than *likely* they'll screw up again. Why? Because many people today are either too busy or too proud to make changes. Or they just don't care. An unfortunate reality. So be wary if you con-tinue to deal with people or entities who have done you wrong. Ask if they've made any adjustments to prevent a repeat. If you don't like the answer, you'd do well to seek alternatives. Why make yourself crazy?

218
Slow your perception of time.

A recent study suggests there are physiological reasons why time appears to pass more quickly for adults than it does for children. Which may explain why the year that seems like a week to an older person is an eternity to a younger one. Still, there are ways you can slow your perception of how fast time is moving (if not the passage of time itself). One is to be in the moment, to focus solely on the activity you're engaged in—without rushing or giving in to distraction. Another is to do what made time seem so boundless to us as kids: take as much of it as you need to explore, observe and savor what interests you most...naturally...without being tied to a schedule. Do that, and maybe the rest of your life won't seem like a mad dash to the finish line. Why make yourself crazy?

219
Don't let outside pressures
run your life.

Everyone today is under unrelenting pressure to do more, spend more, work more, volunteer more, play more. And we give in because we fear being left behind, or people will think ill of us, or we never learned how to say no. In effect, we're handing over the reins of our lives to others...relinquishing control to outside influences oblivious to our own best interests. No wonder we're a crazed society! Sure, there are lots of great things to do out there. But do them selectively. In your own time. At your own pace. And recognize that you simply can't do them all. Resist those outside pressures and follow your own inner compass. Why make yourself crazy?

220
If you don't need to check luggage...don't.

Are you one of those notorious over-packers? Do you feel compelled to cover yourself for just about any contingency? Does most of what you bring along return home untouched? Maybe you don't mind hauling half your wardrobe on a 2-3 day business trip or weekend getaway. But with today's long baggage check-in lines, multilevel security checks, delays at pickup carousels, and the constant threat of lost luggage...it pays to take it on board. For once, let go the urge to over-pack and see if you can't make do with just what you need—neatly tucked into a carry-on, supplemented by a purse or briefcase. Avail yourself of hotel laundry services if necessary. But once you've had a taste of the walk-on/walk-off ease of not checking luggage, you won't want to travel any other way. Why make yourself crazy?

221
Don't deny yourself occasional "sprawl" time.

Sprawl time is that unplanned, spontaneous time when you almost involuntarily disengage from an arduous task to flip through a magazine, lapse into a conversation, putter around aimlessly, or drift off into a reverie. Don't chide yourself on such occasions. Or feel guilty you've put time to no worthwhile purpose. Quite the contrary. Look at these interludes as circuit breakers, telling you to ease up and rest a bit or you'll burn yourself out, become irritable, frustrated, overstressed. Rather than resist, let your mind and body welcome these relaxing breaks from the unrelenting grind. Why make yourself crazy?

222
Don't give out your fax number or email address.

Unless you know who wants it and exactly what they'll be using it for. Otherwise, expect it to be sold, bartered, misused, and distributed to even the most unscrupulous of people. And you'll be the harried victim of relentless spam, junk faxes, duplicitous schemes, or worse—costing you precious time, resources and money, and compromising your security. Unless this information is "required" to complete a transaction, it's none of their business. Why make yourself crazy?

223
Wash a window today.

Windows are among the items we most neglect to clean. Literally, it can result in a dim, hazy, unclear view of the outside. Symbolically, it can cloud your perspective in other ways, too. So today, pick a window—preferably the one you look through most—and wash it. Inside and out, if possible. You'll discover that cleaning a single window is no big deal. But the clear, optimistic view you'll gain will be significant. Tomorrow, maybe clean another one. Before you know it, with seemingly minimal effort, all your windows will be clean. Even better, your outlook will be infinitely brighter. Why make yourself crazy?

224
Ask for help.

Whenever you reach a frustrating impasse—in your work, home projects, business transactions, travel, relationships, or any other area—and you don't know where to turn...ask for help. From friends, associates, professionals, even strangers. If you're too proud to seek assistance, or fear it's a sign of weakness (which it's not), you're only compounding your stress and futility. Most people are more than happy to share their knowledge, wisdom and expertise. Indeed, they welcome the opportunity to show it off. Just don't abuse their generosity or bother them with trivial things you can easily take care of yourself. Know the point where trying to go it alone crosses the line from persevering to pigheaded. Ask for help. Why make yourself crazy?

225
Being a good person doesn't mean being a chump.

Always being nice, agreeable and never making waves isn't necessarily what goodness and honesty are all about. On the contrary, it can signal weakness of resolve, invite disrespect and encourage others to take advantage of you. Sometimes you have to create a little friction to do what's right. And some people aren't going to like it. But that's unavoidable. You do what you must. Goodness isn't a synonym for popularity. It's an adherence to moral principles regardless of what people think. So stop stressing over a need to please everyone. You won't. And will be worse off if you try. Just focusing on being a good person is reward enough in itself. Why make yourself crazy?

226
Cut your teens some slack.

When kids grow into teenagers, they begin to look every bit like adults. So we expect them to act like adults. And when they don't, which is often, it stresses the heck out of us. Ease up a little. Although they're sprouting up and filling out, and their voices are changing, they're still basically children! Else they'd be out living and working on their own, wouldn't they? Accept that your job isn't done yet, by any stretch, and there are many more years of patience and understanding to go through. Yes, give them more responsibility, let them enjoy a taste of adulthood, but expect that they'll make mistakes, express the most infuriating viewpoints, and do the most nonsensical things. They're works in progress. Think how confused and chaotic *your* adolescence was. It will help you stave off, or at least endure, the classic struggle between parent and teen. Why make yourself crazy?

227
Be focused, but not fixated.

Performing a task with steady concentration and pleasant absorption is an ideal working state. But that focus can quickly become obsessive when you hit an obstacle, get frustrated and can't pull yourself away from overcoming it—even when you know you should. The longer you remain fixated, the harder it is to let go and the more frustrated you'll become. Especially if your persistence is causing you to foolishly neglect more pressing needs. Do the smart thing. Cut yourself loose. Put some space between you and the problem. And revisit it later on. Why make yourself crazy?

228
Get lost.

Now don't get offended, I don't mean it that way. Get lost, as in losing yourself so completely in a diversion, you forget about all those other things stressing you out...and realize that they weren't worth agonizing over in the first place. Good ways to get lost are rambling walks, ballgames, movies, museums, books, street fairs, weekends away, or just hopping in your car and going for a leisurely drive. Anything you don't have to plan, fret about or watch the clock during. You'll find these unscheduled interludes are a reality in themselves, not just an escape from it. And that your life needn't always be the restrained and programmed regimen it is. So get lost. Why make yourself crazy?

229
Eat outdoors.

Dining alfresco is one of life's special pleasures. You get the same relaxation bonus whether you're in a restaurant garden, a picnic pavilion, a sidewalk café, or your own backyard. Conversation is more spirited and less formal. The open space is liberating. The atmosphere more festive. The views more interesting. The food tastes better, too, perhaps because the fresh air makes you hungrier. Take every opportunity to enjoy your meals outside. From the moment you're seated, you'll feel your stress just slip away. Why make yourself crazy?

230
Weed your garden. Weed your life.

Literally, yank those sprouting weeds out of the ground. They're unsightly. They tangle, snarl and suppress the growth of wanted plants. And they'll grow wildly out of control if you ignore them. Such is true with the weeds of your life. Like mounting clutter. Excessive activities. Unhealthy situations. Little problems that can grow into big ones if you don't nip them in the bud. And stifle your own growth and happiness. Root them out. Fully and cleanly. You'll feel free, unencumbered and clear-minded. Whack those weeds. Why make yourself crazy?

231
Limit your personal business at work.

Whether you're the boss or the bossed, spending too much job time on your own affairs can leave you tense and guilt-ridden. Not to mention behind in your work. No matter how discreetly you try to get it done, people notice. And some will resent it. Maybe even gripe about it to others. Sure, there's a certain amount of personal stuff everyone does—has to do—which is perfectly acceptable. But you know you've crossed the line when you become anxious, furtive, even defensive about it. Look, work is filled with enough stress already, without having to throw more anxiety into the mix. Most personal things can be taken care of in the off hours anyway. You've got a job to do. Why make yourself crazy?

232
Don't wait for an opportunity.
Create one.

The good jobs, mates, houses, and business ventures don't come knocking. You have to go out and get them. Waiting for the phone to ring, the letter to arrive, the suitor to pop into your life is nerve-wracking futility. And playing it hard-to-get or aloof doesn't cut it either. Someone else will squeeze you out in a heartbeat. Be proactive. Stake out what you want, devise a plan and go after it. Be bold and innovative. And have a Plan B in place, ready to launch, in case you reach a dead end. Don't wait for others to do for you what you can much more ardently do for yourself. Why make yourself crazy?

233
Read yourself to sleep.

Sleepless or restless nights are often caused by everyday stress and anxiety. That's because you're wound up, thinking about things, reliving the day's charged events. You have to get out of that mode. Just lying there in bed, hoping you'll fall asleep, might not do it. This can. Each night, get into a comfortable reading position, turn off the bedroom light and turn on a small booklight, which you've attached to a fairly unexciting book. (Suspense thrillers might have the opposite effect.) This accomplishes two things. It takes your mind off your current concerns. And it lulls you into a drowsy stupor. It may not happen at first. So give it several nights to condition yourself to the routine. Once accustomed, you may find you can barely get through a page before you're down for the count. Give it a try. Why make yourself crazy?

234
Don't lose sleep over losing sleep.

You're lying in bed and can't sleep. So you become upset that you're squandering prime slumber time. Which causes you to lose even more sleep. Which upsets you even more. Before you know it, it's dawn and you're beside yourself. If this happens frequently, professional help may be required. But if it's only an occasional problem caused by a current stressful circumstance, assure yourself of this. While you may not be asleep, you're at least resting your body and mind in a quiet, dark, peaceful environment. You're *not* working, you're *not* burning energy, you're *not* up and about. Resources are being replenished. Use this knowledge to relax and comfort yourself. Take your mind off present concerns. More than likely you'll eventually drift off into sleep. And even if it's only for a little while, view it as needed rest gained. Why make yourself crazy?

235
Stop trying to find meaning in everything.

Don't be agitated or uneasy when you can't fathom a reason for something or where it fits into the overall scheme of things. Some things don't fit anywhere. Or mean anything. Maybe there isn't even an overall scheme. At least not what we imagine it to be. Life is filled with totally senseless, mundane, unremarkable events that defy characterization. And are best left that way. So spare yourself the futility of trying to find an underlying purpose to everything, or to imbue it with significance. They can't all be defining moments. Why make yourself crazy?

236
Don't have a stroke trying to open a package.

There's a competition among manufacturers to see who can make their products the most exasperating to open. And they're all doing a terrific job. What used to be fairly easy can now be infuriating. Vacuum-sealed jar lids could humble Hercules. Blister packs are absolutely impenetrable. Twist-off bottle caps will gouge your fingers. Cellophane snack bags defy pulling apart. First, resign yourself to not being able to enjoy what you bought right away. Then prepare to do battle. Keep a pair of strong scissors handy. (Hedge shears for more brawny containers.) If you're worried about how the package will look if you have to bring it back, don't. It's not your fault. And if the only difference between two brands is the ease of getting it open...well, you know which one to choose. Why make yourself crazy?

237
Don't seek success on the failure of others.

Seek it on your own merit. Trying to gain advantage hoping others will stumble, or waging a campaign to hurt or discredit them, serves only to bring down the level of dignity all around. It engenders negativity, discord and tension. Whatever the area of involvement—job, government, community, or family—everyone should support each other in working toward common ideals. It's counter-productive to wish for things to get worse, just so you can make your case or improve your position. Strive to be an active contributor, not a stealthy detractor. Your success will be more highly regarded when it's an out-growth of excellence, not a byproduct of failure. Why make yourself crazy?

238
It's okay to change your mind.

There's a disturbing trend in today's culture to brand as weak anyone who changes a position on a particular issue. True if your views waver like a blade of grass swaying in the breeze. But if your altered stance is the result of new evidence learned, a key shift in circumstances, or a serious grappling with the issue, you have every right to change your mind. In fact, it's a sign of strength and maturity to do so in the face of possible criticism. Indeed, it's those whose pride and ego prevent them from abandoning failed positions who should be deemed weak. Don't let any-one belittle you or discourage you from switching viewpoints. Firmly state that you now see things dif-ferently, you've changed your mind and that's that. Why make yourself crazy?

239
Rent a funny movie tonight.

A previous tip extolled the remarkable ability of laughter to relieve stress. But if you find it difficult to see any humor in your current life circumstances, try a wholesale infusion. Rent one of your all-time favorite funny movies that you know for certain will provide a few belly laughs. Note how readily it eases tension, dissipates anxiety, lightens your mood and outlook. It's a great Rx for stress. Repeat as necessary. You'll realize that the funniest stuff is based on real-life situations anyway. And thus you may begin to see some of the humor in yours. Why make yourself crazy?

240
Jot down your questions.

Whenever you have important questions to ask of someone—doctor, lawyer, salesperson, instructor, supervisor, contractor, whomever—write them all down. It's very easy to forget additional questions beyond the first one, and you may not get the opportunity to ask again anytime soon. Or arduously have to track down the person a second time. Also, think about possible follow-up questions you might have if an answer goes a certain way. Many professionals today are too busy to volunteer information. You have to grill it out of them. You're paying for their expertise. Make sure you get it. Why make yourself crazy?

241
Enjoy the stress-reducing effects of mind travel.

Physically removing yourself from a stressful environment with a night out, weekend away or a real vacation is the ideal escape. But when that isn't possible, indulge in a stress-releasing mind trip. Close your eyes and imagine someplace you'd truly love to be: beach, mountains, woods, resort, island...any visualized setting that calms you down. Try not to force it or focus too hard, but take a more relaxed daydream approach, letting the details fill themselves in. As your stress eases, you'll see how effective the power of suggestion can be. When your mind travels, there are no budget restrictions, reservations to make, passports required, or tickets to purchase. Go where you want, whenever you want and do what you wish. Bon voyage. Why make yourself crazy?

242
Don't let others leave you in limbo.

There are people you know who keep changing plans on you. Or whose inability to decide on something is holding you up. Or who aren't giving you the whole story. And it's usually for their own benefit, with little regard for yours. It's nice to be accommodating. To a point. But when another's vacillating is hanging you up, stressing you out...it's time to get firm. Have no qualms about saying "I've got to move on this." "I need an answer." Or "I have to know, one way or the other." It will jolt them into an awareness that you have needs, too. And help them get off the dime. Don't be a patsy for another's indecision. Why make yourself crazy?

243
Inundated with paper? Get rid of it!

The paperless society is a fairytale. There's more paper cluttering our lives than ever. Newspapers, flyers, faxes, photocopies, handouts, documents, receipts, printouts, magazines, brochures, letters, shopping bags, wrapping paper... It's piling up all over the place. And if you don't keep pace, it will devour you. Most of it is worthless to you anyway. So recycle it. And cut off the flow. Don't collect free literature you aren't going to read. Clean out a file every day. Beg off mailing lists. Make digital copies instead of hard copies of computer-generated documents and print out only when necessary. Spare yourself the aggravation of runaway paper clutter. You'll save a few trees, too. Why make yourself crazy?

244
Spend more time outdoors.

Many who are stressed out spend a lot of time penned in. They have sedentary occupations—chained to computers, desks and enclosed work areas. Their jobs afford little physical activity and scant opportunity to get out during the day. That oppressiveness can amplify stress and job pressure. If you're in that boat, the last thing you need are evenings and weekends cooped up inside. Offset the hemmed-in feeling of your workday with energetic outdoor activities like tennis, golf, biking, walks, hikes, or even more adventurous pursuits. On your lunch breaks, get away from your desk, go outside and at least grab a lungful of fresh air. It'll make a noticeable difference. Adults need recess, too. Get out and play. Why make yourself crazy?

245
Set aside time for each other.

Are you too busy to be a husband? Wife? Lover? Relationships often get shortchanged in the hubbub of daily life. In fact, they're usually first to get tossed aside, often to make room for the most insignificant things. That's taking each other way too much for granted. You risk letting your intimacy fade and your relationship wither. Keep both well nourished. Set aside a chunk of time each week to spend together, just the two of you. Make it inviolable, mandatory, and go out and have a good time. Strong relationships stay strong by building in essential time for each other. Why short-change yourself? Why make yourself crazy?

246
Don't fret over looming, stressful events.

You have to undergo a medical procedure, give a speech, meet your future in-laws, fire your assistant, fly on an airplane, compete in an important game. Fretting about it will only make you live through a negative outcome over and over...before it even or ever happens! Block out those bad thoughts and dwell on the overwhelming odds everything will turn out just fine. (Even if you do lose the game.) Why make yourself crazy?

247
Beware of one-sided relationships.

Whether a friend or lover, when it's all give and no take, one person gets saddled with all the responsibilities, all the maintenance of the relationship. If that's you, it means you're carrying the burden for both of you. And not only is it unfair, it's unduly stressful. Examine your relationships closely, as you may not even be aware it's happening. But if you detect a pattern where *you* are always the one being leaned on, making the plans, picking up the tab, or stepping in to help the other—with little or no giveback or gratitude—a change is in order. Maybe it's confronting the issue directly, seeking counseling or severing ties altogether. It's one thing to help someone, quite another to be used insensitively. Why make yourself crazy?

248
Don't like the mood of
a group? Change it.

When the tone of a social gathering becomes too confrontational, negative, lewd, insensitive, prejudiced, or otherwise distasteful, you needn't remain at the mercy of it. It takes nerve, but speak up, intercede, try to steer things back into positive territory. Offenders may be taken aback, even disdainful, but those who share your discomfort will welcome the intervention. Too often we let situations deteriorate beyond what we find acceptable and may be hesitant to address it. But silence only helps to condone the behavior. Try to defuse the bad vibes. And if you can't, make a statement by politely excusing yourself and leaving. Why make yourself crazy?

249
Just listen to yourself.

Listen to the way you huff and groan from the minute you wake up till the time you turn in. Hear yourself gripe about the most miniscule things, eager to express disapproval or lodge a complaint at the drop of a hat. Eavesdrop on your inner voice as it finds fault in everything, silently cussing people, systems, rules, and glitches throughout the day. We all do this to some extent. And it erodes our sense of well-being and composure. Every time you get the urge to be cross, think of the real sufferings people endure around the world. It's a humbling exercise. Just listen to yourself. And trade in your sighs of annoyance for the oohs and ahs of opportunity, discovery and gratitude. Why make yourself crazy?

250
If only you had more money...

Wealth would solve everything, wouldn't it? No more stress...able to take care of any problem in a flash...people fawning all over you. Everything would be easy, right? Pure bliss. At least, that's how we may see it from our vantage point. Truth be told, wealth comes with its own stresses, pressures and pitfalls. Bring them on, you say? Fair enough. But just be aware that while there are many happy rich people, there are also many miserable ones. Just as there are joyous people who are dirt poor. So it's not always the money. And if you're living a crazed life now with the expectation that wealth will change all that, you may be disappointed. The thing to do is free yourself of the stress now. You'll indeed be richer in a lot of ways. And in the event you do become wealthy, you'll know a lot better how to handle it. Why make yourself crazy?

251
Forget about deadlines.
How about startlines?

For a society so obsessed with when a project gets finished, we're curiously all too casual about when to get it started. And that can be the most critical factor of all. Which may explain why so many deadlines aren't met. Instead of stressing over when something is due, focus on getting it underway. Set a "startline." That is, a time before which it's essential you get a project started, so it isn't performed in a rushed and slapdash manner. If you stick to your startline, it not only assures efficient, unhurried performance, it all but eliminates the need for a deadline...and the anxiety that goes with it. Which "line" would you rather work under? Get it started. Why make yourself crazy?

252
Write your troubles away.

Keep a journal. Diary. Blog. Whatever you want to call it. You don't have to write a lot each day...or even every day. And it needn't be a tedious play-by-play of your life. Record unusual incidents, hurts and gripes, triumphs and failures, reflections, rants, hilarity, disappointment...anything you feel compelled to vent. Scrawl it into a notebook, or tap it out on your computer. It doesn't really matter. Just getting it out is the object. You'll feel better every time you do it. And when you come back to it years later, you'll open a fascinating window into your past. Like spying on another person. You'll learn a great deal from it, too. Writing a five or ten minute entry can be a healthy release. Why make yourself crazy?

253
Don't trust yourself when you're upset.

You're furious at someone. Flustered by an embarrassing thing you did. Or upset about a serious blunder you made. In that distressed state, you're unfocused, distracted, likely to make costly errors and thus compound the misery you're feeling. In those situations, it's wise to consciously slow down and proceed with caution, as if navigating a ship through perilous waters. Even better, don't attempt anything important or complicated until you've had a chance to calm and collect yourself. You can't see clearly when you're seeing red. Why make yourself crazy?

254
Don't act out confrontations in your head.

What angry scenes we stage in our minds! Reenactments of arguments recently fought. Vengeful thoughts of what we'll say next time we see that so-and-so. Seething dialogs and envisioned acts of retribution aimed at whatever current nemesis we're up against. These inner rants can poison your temperament, and have an all-consuming effect far out of proportion to whatever caused it. Become skilled at sidestepping these ill feelings before they have a chance to devour you. Let things play out in reality, rather than your mind. You'll find they usually resolve themselves a lot more peacefully than you imagined. Allowing yourself to get worked up only fuels your ire again and again. It isn't worth it. Why make yourself crazy?

255
Be a good gear switcher.

You may have the kind of job, or life, where you constantly have to drop something to take care of something else. This can be a never-ending source of stress and frustration. If you let it. Or, as unlikely as it seems now, you can condition yourself to get used to it...even enjoy it! When you prepare yourself for such interruptions, you can make a clean break without anxiety, knowing you'll return later on to tie up loose ends. Just give whatever you're doing at the moment your undivided focus...and let it go promptly when necessary. Quick transitioning is a skill, an art you can learn, master and take satisfaction in. Why make yourself crazy?

256
Be your own best pal.

Are you comfortable when you're by yourself? Can you do things solo and enjoy them—like going to the movies, a restaurant, museum, even traveling—without feeling ill at ease or self-conscious? Or do you always feel you have to have someone else in tow, and lacking that are prone to miss out? If so, be assertive, take the initiative and do more things on your own. You'll find it liberating, stress-reducing and confidence-building. And the more comfortable you grow with yourself, the less timid you'll become, and the farther your horizons will span. When a companion isn't available, be your own best pal. Why make yourself crazy?

257
Tough out the stress of big transitions.

Everything is going along at an even keel, sometimes even for years, when suddenly...you're starting a new job. Moving. Getting married. Having a baby. Going off to school. Making a major life transition. That means a lot of planning, doing and upheaval in a compressed amount of time. The stress can be intense, unrelenting. Endure it with the knowledge that while it may be daunting, it's only temporary. Use the prospect of new and exciting things to get past the current turmoil. And have faith that the bumps will soon even out and your life will once again assume a level of normalcy. Why make yourself crazy?

258
Put affection back into your relationship.

A small amount of affection can melt days, months, even years of tension, distance and discord between you and your partner. Take the initiative, swallow your pride and rekindle the affection you once thrived on. A reassuring hand on the shoulder, a simple kiss, a gentle hug are good places to start. Keep at it, even if it's not immediately returned or acknowledged. In time a thaw will take hold, and warmth and intimacy likely ensue. A daily dose of affection can often soothe what words can't. Why make yourself crazy?

259
Don't deny yourself the benefits of massage.

It's a pity more people don't partake in the numerous advantages of massage therapy. Perhaps your reluctance is the expense, a feeling of modesty or the sense that massage is overindulgent and pampering. Hardly the case. Studies show that massage reduces your heart rate, lowers blood pressure, increases circulation and lymph flow, relaxes muscles, makes you more alert and able to work more efficiently, and reduces stress, anxiety and tension. Reason enough? If you're shy about visiting a professional masseuse (and you shouldn't be, since it's their job to make you feel comfortable!), or it doesn't fit into your budget, try trading massages with your partner. Few things can better allay the tensions of a long, hard day. Why make yourself crazy?

260
Schedule things now you can enjoy later on.

If you don't plan leisurely pursuits now for down the road, you'll never get to do the things you really want to and should be doing. Take the initiative. Buy tickets for shows, concerts and sporting events weeks, even months in advance. Enroll now in a fun and interesting class you'll take next semester. Get family and friends on your calendar for future activities before their schedules fill up. And book weekend getaways far ahead. You'll feel your stress lift just by doing this. And will enjoy the prospect of it all the while. The best part is, when the time comes, it's all planned and paid for. You simply pick up and go! Be good to yourself. Plan now. Because you'll never find the openings in your wall-to-wall regimen later on. Why make yourself crazy?

261
Don't drive while distracted.

And I know many do. But when you're talking on your cell phone, putting on makeup, eating breakfast, or (not uncommon) READING!—while operating a multi-ton motor vehicle—you're putting yourself and others in danger. For basically naught. Studies show, whether you're driving or not, multi-tasking is less effective, less productive than doing things sequentially. Why? Because you're not doing either task well. Plus, it's stressful, so you're burning nervous energy—energy you won't have when you need it later on. Still not convinced? A recent study shows that the constant distractions of multitasking destroys cells in the hippocampus. It's frying your brain! So be safe. Drive focused. Why make yourself crazy?

262
Have more fun in bed.

So advised a popular mattress ad. And they had a point. You don't need a study (like the one mentioned below) to tell you that a healthy sex life can reduce stress. As much as a lack of sex can aggravate it. But today, with our busy schedules and relentless ambitions, sex for many couples has become little more than an afterthought. Sometimes overlooked entirely. This is obviously unhealthy for the relationship. Which adds to even greater stress. Now, the study. According to the Royal Hospital in Edinburgh, a healthy sex life can make you look up to seven years younger, lead to greater contentment and help you sleep better. Why argue? Light the candle, draw the shades and... Why make yourself crazy?

263
Take a warm, relaxing bath.

How long has it been? Have you forgotten that bathtubs aren't just places to stand while you're taking a shower? Or how soothing and restorative a good soak can be? Tonight, draw yourself a nice toasty bath. Add beads, bubbles and toys as needed. Allow your body to relax and your mind to drift. This is a stress remedy that has worked like a charm for thousands of years! And about the only downside is having to get out. Got stress? Jump in the tub. Why make yourself crazy?

264
Open your mind to new things.

Part of what keeps us locked into stress mode is the feeling we have no alternatives, that it's impossible to break away from our indentured lives of tension and pressure. "Maybe someone else, but not me" is the self-perpetuating attitude. Sure, we entertain thoughts of changing our ways, but it usually goes no further than fantasy. It takes risk, it takes courage to break through the mental barriers into new territory. But once you do this, all sorts of possibilities open up...and your resistance to them eases. Next time you get a chance to experience life in new and different ways—and unburden yourself of anxiety and stress— grab it. You may never get that opportunity again. Why make yourself crazy?

265
Judge what they do, not what they say.

People have become masters at artfully deceptive, duplicitous use of language. They can steal you blind and make you feel they've done something wonderful for you. Very often we're no match for the verbal gymnastics of politicians, sales people and others who make their living at this. Even so-called friends and lovers can put one over on you before you even know what's happening. So don't put much stock in what people are saying, look carefully at what they are doing. Determine what the net effect on you is, without being waltzed by the elaborate words it comes packaged in. By learning to see past the innumerable spins, twists and shadings of the truth, you can spare yourself a lot of bad choices and disappointment. Why make yourself crazy?

266
Have a legitimate excuse
to get off the phone.

How stressful are phone calls that drag on far longer than they need to! And in our honesty, we're usually reluctant to fabricate the white lie that will end them. To avoid this: when calling people or scheduling them to call you, have a built-in time limit already in place. For example, schedule the call 10 or 15 minutes before you have to go into a meeting, pick up the kids or leave for an appointment. That way you have a truthful, inarguable excuse to cut it short. And don't feel guilty doing this repeatedly to the same person (we all know at least one). It's a subtle way of delivering the message that your time is valuable...and not open-ended. Why make yourself crazy?

267
Work at what you love.

You'll never work more willingly, passionately and tirelessly than when you work at something you love. Don't deny yourself this ultimate satisfaction—even if you have to start in your spare time, even if you're not at first making money at it. The enthusiasm and energy you bring to a favorite endeavor might all but ensure its success, and in time it may even become your primary occupation. Or, you may decide that a reduced income is more than compensated by the happiness it brings to your life. At the very least, try to get past the thinking stages and start putting your dreams into action. Anything is possible. Why make yourself crazy?

268
Don't operate on an empty stomach.

Sometimes in your dogged adhesion to the tasks at hand, you'll let yourself go far too long without eating. Or skip a meal entirely. Usually it's breakfast or lunch that gets scuttled. But continuing to perform while hungry can make you irritable, dejected, resentful, stressed. If it's impossible to pull yourself away, or mealtime is hours off, at least keep healthy snack foods handy. A little bit of munching on the fly can take the edge off your hunger...and turn your temperament entirely around. Why make yourself crazy?

269
Don't tolerate being shouted at.

As if you haven't noticed, the world has become a more shrill, loud and aggressive place. Everyone wants your attention, money or aid, and they aren't concerned about disrupting your peace and harmony to get it. Don't allow them. When a news reporter delivers a story with blaring sensationalism...switch channels. When radio and TV ads assault you with boisterous insensitivity...tune them out. When family members or coworkers voice their wants with inconsiderate loudness, turn a deaf ear until they can address you with civility. Points can be argued, wishes conveyed, products sold, and news reported...without having to subject you to stressful shouting. Demand better. Why make yourself crazy?

270
Don't give out knee-jerk invitations.

For instance, those insincere, spur-of-the-moment utterances like "I'd really like to have you over sometime." The ones that may serve the moment, and you think sound magnanimous, but you have little intention of following up on soon. They're usually met with skepticism and make the other person feel awkward, since how is one supposed to respond to such disingenuous ambiguity? Besides, the unfulfilled promises you make just add to the uneasiness and stress in your life. Another empty offer: "Next time you're in the neighborhood, stop by." Few today are going to take that risk. Either call people up and invite them over with a specific date, time and purpose in mind...or don't say anything at all. Why make yourself crazy?

271
Don't be a short order cook.

How much of your time, energy and composure is squandered every night making multiple meals for your family? Trying to cater to every taste by preparing different dishes is okay if you're a restaurant, but a needless burden otherwise. Unless someone has a food allergy or intolerance, adopt a policy of one meal for the entire family. And stick to it. Make a master list of all the foods everyone likes. If you aren't sure, ask. Let good nutrition rule. Encourage finicky eaters to try new things by not spoiling them with alternatives. Or prepare foods in ways more palatable to them (like pouring melted cheese over broccoli). Experiment with new recipes and note what works. A little reconnaissance up front can pay off in fewer culinary squabbles and less stressful evenings down the line. One family, one meal. Why make yourself crazy?

272
Dine by candlelight.

Turn the lights down low, light a candle, put on some soft music, and turn an ordinary dinner into a relaxing escape. Let the natural, mesmerizing effects of the lambent flame soothe and comfort you. Conversation becomes more genial and intimate. Tensions slip away. A little candlelight can change the entire complexion of your evening. Avail yourself frequently of its stress-easing allure. Why make yourself crazy?

273
Are you suffering from "indecisionitis"?

Do you reach a point where you have so many things to do you can't do anything at all? Are you pulled in so many different directions you're virtually paralyzed? Do you dawdle aimlessly and become deflated because you're afraid that committing yourself to one project means neglecting another equally important one? Then you have indecisionitis. A common affliction of the stressed and overscheduled. When it happens, your inaction can feed on itself and lead to an increasingly upsetting crisis. Realize this: doing something, anything, is better than nothing at all. So force yourself to get started on a project just to break the logjam, to ease the pressure on yourself. Accept that you're only human, only one person and at such times something's got to give. Why make yourself crazy?

274
Do you have any idea what stress is doing to you?

Constant, everyday stress unleashes free radicals and harmful hormones; weakens your immune system; puts you at greater risk for cancer, heart disease, diabetes, and stroke; ages you prematurely; contributes to sleeplessness and weight problems; makes you tense, anxious and irritable; strains your relationships; causes unreliable work performance and job dissatisfaction; promotes poor judgment, mistakes and accidents; and robs you of happiness and peace of mind. Sadly, stress has become the permissible pathogen. It is too widely tolerated, even perversely esteemed as symbolic of a strong work ethic. These attitudes must be challenged. It's insanity to keep subjecting yourself to the ravages of stress. You have the power to change that. *Use it.* Why make yourself crazy?

275
Look beyond appearances to find the good in people.

How callously we judge others based solely on superficial qualities! What someone wears, how they talk, where they live, or what they drive has little to do with their underlying goodness and the emotions they feel. But in our rushed and impatient dealings—to our detriment—we hastily slot people into categories and judge them accordingly. Think of all the people you're intimate with today you first estimated unfairly, maybe even joked about, based on outward appearances. Imagine what you'd have lost...and lose every day... when you can't get beyond stereotyping. The easiest way to accept others is to know them, to discover the person inside. You'll find that inwardly most people share similar beliefs and aspirations. You want others to understand who *you* are. At least afford them the same courtesy. Why make yourself crazy?

276
Do more shopping online.

Not to knock conventional shopping, since for many it's actually a way to relieve stress. Especially since you don't have to buy anything to enjoy getting out and browsing your favorite stores. But when shopping becomes an arduous necessity and you have little time to spare, the Internet can be a lifesaver. Use it to scout out available brands and products, research features and benefits, comparison price shop, get objective product reviews, and narrow down your choices. Even if you end up making the purchase in a store, you can cut your time and effort dramatically by doing the legwork online. Today, you can find just about anything you want on the Web. Why make yourself crazy?

277
Remember: you're one in 7 billion.

So solving the problems of the world doesn't rest solely on your shoulders. (Although it sometimes may seem that way.) And with all those people out there, it's a cinch there's going to be a conflict somewhere at any given time. And a few people are going to go a little haywire now and then. That's what makes the headlines, not the billions of people who live relatively quiet, law-abiding lives. If you view the world through the unforgiving eye of the media, of course doomsday is always going to seem just outside your door. But it isn't so. Pull back and put things in their rightful perspective. In fact, the amazing reality is, most of us 7 billion get along pretty well. Why make yourself crazy?

278
Let answers unfold.

Every day you have questions. Lots of them. Like: How will I get this done? What should I do about so-and-so? How will this affect me? Where am I headed?

So many questions. And not having ready answers can be unnerving, ever leaving you hanging. First, acknowledge that you will always have questions. Because as soon as they're answered others present themselves. But rather than run around frantically trying to find quick answers, let them unfold naturally. When you do this, you not only relieve a lot of stress, the answers you get will more often be the right ones. Few things need to be resolved immediately. Let your questions steep a while. The answers will inevitably materialize. Why make yourself crazy?

279
Be a proponent of civility.

The veneer of civility is very thin. It must be protected like the fragile ozone layer. It doesn't take much dissension or stress to shatter good will and kindness among people. As it is, vulgar language, bad taste, rudeness, insensitive treatment, and crude behavior are slowly overspreading our culture. And this loss of propriety aggravates the tensions we feel every day. We've come too far as a civilization to let others drag us back into a base and thoughtless existence. Be civil. And promote civility. Why make yourself crazy?

280
Be aware of your surroundings.

If your mind is miles away from where you are and what you're doing at the moment—whether driving, shopping or just being out and about—your detachment can be a risk to you. These are the times when wallets are left on store counters, highway exits are missed, appointments are forgotten, and people become targets for pickpockets...or worse. Having too much on your plate, and your mind, divides your attention and makes you prone to mishaps and mistakes—which will leave you even more unhinged. Learn to push your distractions aside and concentrate on giving each activity in its turn the presence of mind it demands. Why make yourself crazy?

281
Don't take sides when it
doesn't concern you.

Stay neutral, if you can, in office politics, family squabbles and interpersonal bickering. It'll save you a world of unnecessary aggravation and trouble. People try to recruit allies for even their most petty disputes, and will eagerly drag you into the fray to help fight their battles. Don't let them. Rise above it. Listen attentively and objectively to both sides, offer your suggestions, but stay on the sidelines. You've got your own issues to worry about, without having to take on everyone else's. Why make yourself crazy?

282
Who cares what they say?

You can often measure the success of people by the shrillness of their detractors. Note that those who are steadfast and persevering do not cave in to criticism. On the contrary, they gain strength from it. If you're taking the heat for trying to live a simpler, saner life, when some would prefer you continue to accompany them on a daily dance of chaos, don't give in. This is a true test of your willingness to live for yourself. What others say, what others think should not be of consequence. Why make yourself crazy?

283
Pump some iron.

Not necessarily in a body building way, but in a muscle stretching, circulation boosting, stress reducing way. Most occupations today leave our bodies limp and flaccid. To remain the physically robust, sharp-thinking beings we evolved to be, we have to frequently work out. Best to use the weight-adjustable exercise machines and circuits found at health clubs, gyms and hotels. Or try free weights at home. Start with safer, lighter weights and work your way up over time. (There's no point in pushing it.) And try to exercise all the muscle groups. You'll not only feel great, you'll find that stress has little place to hide in a healthy body. Take it from Arnold. Lose those jelly bellies. Firm up the thighs. Why make yourself crazy?

284
Have a night out with the guys...or girls.

Spending free time with the family understandably is a top priority. But every now and then it's smart stress management to indulge in a boys' night out or a girls' night out. You relax and unwind in different ways when you socialize with members of the same sex. You can talk more openly than you do in mixed company. You can loosen up, laugh and be less formal. There are numerous excuses for getting together: sports, card games, book discussions, eating out...or for no other reason than to enjoy each other's company. And don't wait for it to happen. Be the instigator. Today, with email, it's really easy to set these things up. Both you and your partner should encourage each other to do this on a regular basis. You really need it. Why make yourself crazy?

285
Find your rhythm each day.

Some days you're out of sync with yourself. For example, your brain is lagging behind your body, so you become clumsy, klutzy, blundering into things before you've had a chance to think about them. Sometimes it's the opposite: you're way ahead mentally but you just can't rally yourself to the task physically. Or maybe your mood is way out of whack with that of the group or situation you're dealing with. Let it go no further. Stop. Call a timeout with yourself. Get a fix on where you're amiss. Then consciously make adjustments. Slow down or speed up to get your body in sync with your mind. Alter your temperament so it falls into the orbit of the prevailing mood. This may take an initial thrust of effort, but it can put you on the right track for the rest of the day. Why make yourself crazy?

286
Never be embarrassed at having to scale back.

Unfortunately, we often judge ourselves on the basis of our success or failure. So it can be a blow to your self-esteem if career or financial setbacks force you to abandon a lifestyle, scuttle future plans or cut back on amenities you once took for granted. Don't take it so personally. Even the Donald Trumps of the world stumble now and then. Yet you don't see them writhing in humiliation, do you? So why should *you*? View this as an opportunity to at long last simplify, unburden yourself of stressful baggage, refocus on those who are truly important to you. It's not about your pride and ego. It's about rationally adjusting to the inevitable ebb and flow of life. Why make yourself crazy?

287
Develop mental toughness.

How mentally tough are you? How easily do you give in to peevishness, sulking, low morale, pessimism, and defeat? It isn't enough to be mentally tough only when your mood suits it. On the contrary, it's when you're weak-minded and vulnerable that you most need to rally strength and resilience. Not easy by any stretch. First, monitor yourself to see how readily you cave in to difficult circumstances. Then vow to address them in a different way—as opportunities to respond to challenge, to build up your mental toughness. You'll soon be able to handle almost anything. Adversity? Bring it on. Why make yourself crazy?

288
Don't feel guilty when you can't always give.

You're besieged with requests to give money. To charities, schools, churches, community groups, political organizations, fundraising events... You're solicited by mail, email, telephone, fax, ads, neighbors, co-workers, strangers. Each may be a worthy cause in itself, but collectively the relentless demands can drive you nuts—if not into debt. Sure, you should give. As generously as yours means allow. But give selectively to those causes you feel most passionate about. And the ones you can't afford, don't let yourself, or anyone else, make you feel guilty about. You can't be responsible for all the ills of the world. You do what you can. So never fret over keeping those free return-address stickers or greeting cards, even if you didn't give. Why make yourself crazy?

289
Take no nonsense from surly food servers.

The last thing you need when you're anticipating the pleasant diversion of dining out is a waiter or waitress who gives you grief, tries to rush you out, or ignores you altogether. All the more aggravating be-

cause you're *paying* for such treatment! This is not
the time to suck it up and bite your tongue. Ask to
see the manager and request a new server. If the restaurant can't or won't deliver, it's time to leave. You've
got enough stress to contend with without having it
dragged into your precious leisure time. Why make
yourself crazy?

290
Drink plenty of water.

After oxygen, water is the most vital nutrient. It
plays a role in almost every major body function, including regulating body temperature, carrying nutrients
to cells, removing waste and toxins, cushioning joints,
protecting organs and tissues. Stress further increases
the need for water, the lack of which contributes to
even more stress. Yet most people continually stay de-
hydrated by consuming too little water... and too many
caffeinated and alcoholic beverages that actually *rob*
the body of water. Dehydration also causes fatigue,
confusion, forgetfulness, and rapid breathing. On aver-
age, drink about eight 8-oz servings of water per day.
Sounds like a lot, but it's less than the 2-1/2 quarts we
lose daily under normal circumstances, much less
stressful ones. No wonder we always feel like wilted ge-

raniums! Stay hydrated and stay healthy. Why make yourself crazy?

291
Vote!

There's a bumper sticker that says: "Vote. Or shut up." Blunt, but true. You can't complain about the government if you don't even take the minimal political step of voting. Even if your guy doesn't get in, or a referendum you support is denied, you can at least relieve some of the frustration of feeling powerless when you cast a ballot. You're making a statement. And you won't have to live with the discomfort of having shunned the process. If you're perennially disappointed in political outcomes, maybe you should get even more involved. As it is, rain, cold and long lines are no excuse. Get out and vote. Then marvel as the amazing political institution called democracy plays itself out. Why make yourself crazy?

292
Know the right time to bring up an issue.

Timing is everything, especially when it comes to broaching subjects that are not dear to another's heart, or asking someone to do something for you.

Knowing the right moment can save a lot of unnecessary friction and more easily accomplish your goal. For
example, don't clobber someone with your problems
the minute they walk through the door. Don't ask for
something when a person is clearly up to his neck.
Don't try to talk to someone when they're on the telephone, or interrupt them when they're stressfully engaged. Learn to judge a person's mood and receptivity
before you bring up a sensitive subject or make your
request. It takes practice, but try putting yourself in
the other's position and imagine the best time *you*
would want to be approached. Then follow those instincts. Why make yourself crazy?

293
Be prepared.

For virtually anything. Planning ahead saves time,
makes you more efficient and productive, and mini-
mizes anxiety and doubt. Prepare yourself for the *unexpected*, too, and be accepting of it when it happens.
Things often play out chaotically because people just
aren't ready. Do you want your life to be a litany of
rushed, marred, unpredictable, loose-ended episodes?
Or smooth, well-planned, fully satisfying outcomes?
Then be prepared. Why make yourself crazy?

294
Take frequent breaks.

There's no glory in drudgery. Nor is it fun or satisfying. Break up tedious assignments into smaller
tasks. Pause and get away from the work periodically.
Insert other lighter activities in between. Each time
you come back you'll feel fresh and energized. And
before you know it, your project will be finished. Why
make yourself crazy?

295
Are you a checkaholic?

How much time do you waste excessively checking
things. Check the weather. Check the time. Check the
markets. Check your email. Check your hair. Check
your voicemail. Check the news. Check your makeup.
Check to see if your wallet is still in your pocket. How
much of your day are you frittering away doing this?
More than you might care to know. Ease up. Things
aren't going to fall apart when you're not looking. So
resist the urge to receive constant, needless, monotonous updates. Use that time to maintain your focus...
get more done...or simply take a break. Check frequently on the baby, yes. But everything else? Just
let it go. Why make yourself crazy?

296
Don't believe for a minute...

...you'll get the number of servings the recipe says you will...you can perform a complex computer task with a single click of the mouse...your call is important to them...the "push here on red" button will get you across the street any faster...you're indispensable to your company...your cake will look anything like the one illustrated on the box...the battery will last anywhere near what they claim... Get smart. Lower your expectations. Be prepared for a letdown. Why make yourself crazy?

297
Don't dwell on your discomforts.

Yes, the shower may be too cold, the theater too warm, the guy sitting next to you reeks, the restaurant is noisy, your airplane seat is cramped... Rather than keep reminding yourself how unpleasant you feel, try enveloping yourself in an imaginary buffer. The irritant may still be there, you're vaguely aware of it, but it's not penetrating the mental barrier you've constructed. You're zoned out. Your thoughts are elsewhere, positive and optimistic. Work on this technique. You'll get so good at it you'll be able to slip into your unfazed mode at will...and tune out even the most persistent annoyances. Why make yourself crazy?

298
Don't deliver ultimatums.

They're usually far harsher than the behavior that prompted them...and delivered in a fit of emotion when you're little prepared to make good on them. And if you do, it often hurts you more than the other person—actions you'll almost certainly regret. Conversely, if you back away from your ultimatum, you lose all worthwhile credibility. Your bluff has been called. So instead of threatening to walk out on your lover, quit your job, or cut off your children's inheritance...skip the tough talk, stay cool, think rationally, and inevitably you'll come up with a more prudent, less stressful solution. Why make yourself crazy?

299
Create your own confidence.

So much of stress is caused by a lack of confidence. You're not sure you'll get the job done, win over the other person, learn a skill, make the deadline, deliver a good presentation, close the sale, become a success. And that faltering of confidence in itself can be a major contributor to your failure. Break out of that mindset. Even when you don't feel confident, *act confident*. Yes, fake it. Because in one of the quirks of human nature, false confidence will soon transform itself into real confidence. If you don't believe it, try it. It works. That's how people with little else going for them can be highly successful. And if they can do it, think what you can achieve! All it takes is confidence—real or imagined—to bring it off. Why make yourself crazy?

300
Don't be a sucker for "I'm sorry."

Very likely, the two words in the English language most often spoken with insincerity are "I'm sorry." People toss the phrase about as if it's all they have to do to make amends and wipe the record clean. And they frequently express it with such shallow indifference...even an edge of annoyance! So don't get all worked up over whether or not someone apologizes. It's usually meaningless anyway. Instead, judge individuals on their attempts at retribution—that is, their efforts to make up for what they did in some way. On the flip side, be aware of how often you, too, casually resort to an unfelt "I'm sorry." Taking sincere responsibility for our actions is one way we can relieve tensions in the world. Why make yourself crazy?

301
If every morning is a mad dash...*get up earlier!*

How often we hear the complaint, "I never have enough time in the morning." Duh...*make* time. Simply wake up earlier. Leave yourself ample time to dress, eat a nutritious breakfast and get off to where you're going...sanely. It will set a composed, rational pace for the entire day. But, you say, I like that extra 15 minutes sleep. Well, that added snooze time will cost you big all day long. Get it on the other end. Break the insidious cycle of rushing by retiring early and getting up early, with a good night's sleep in between. Why make yourself crazy?

302
Do you wake up with fear?

Many people do. The minute they open their eyes they face the day with trepidation, out of all context with reality, perhaps influenced by an eerie dream. Don't let this undeserving emotion hijack your mood for the day. Replace gloomy thoughts immediately with optimistic ones, knowing your mind can entertain only one thought at a time. Notice, too, how the feeling of dread dissipates as you shake off sleep and start addressing your needs of the day. So get things going right away and you can erase those unwelcome apprehensions at the outset. Why make yourself crazy?

303
Take naps.

This may run counter to today's misguided work ethic, but several studies have found that people are a lot more productive (and undoubtedly more pleasant) when they take afternoon naps. A twenty-minute to half-hour siesta can work wonders (no longer or it might interfere with your night's sleep). Darn the naysayers. Close the door, have a pleasant snooze, and reap the benefits. Why make yourself crazy?

304
Don't live and die with the financial markets.

If you've invested long-term—and have no intention of cashing in anytime soon—ignore the day-to-day fluctuations of the market. They'll have little bearing on the final tally, but will exact a costly toll in dashed hopes or inflated expectations every time the market dives or soars. Don't become a ticker-tape junkie. Forget about your investments, like gold socked away in a vault. Why make yourself crazy?

305
Get over it.

So you're late. You lost the game. You got a spot on your suit. It cost $350 to fix the car. You missed your favorite show. Will it make a whit of difference a year from now? A week from now? Stop agonizing and get on with it. Factor in these disruptions as a part of life, not exceptions to it. As opportunities to respond to adversity. And if they don't happen, it's gravy. Why make yourself crazy?

306
Don't feel guilty losing touch with people.

You could spend the rest of your life trying to keep up with all the people you've grown close to over the years. Nice if it was possible, but unnecessary and impractical. Accept that those you no longer associate with, or have moved away, will soon fall out of your loop. As undoubtedly you will theirs. And that's okay. Perhaps someday you'll get together. Perhaps not. In any case, at least you'll have each other's memories. So don't be down on yourself, or fault the other person, for drifting apart. It's only natural. Why make yourself crazy?

307
Don't buy what you really don't need.

Before you buy anything, ask yourself two questions. One: do I really need this? And two: could I put this purchase off another week, month, year? If you're honest with yourself, you'll be surprised at how many purchases you can delay or avoid altogether; even better, how much money you can save. And you'll realize how perfectly well you can get by with what you already have. Why make yourself crazy?

308
Don't worry until you have something to worry about.

Maybe you're the type of person who, when things are going great, begins to fret some unforeseen calamity will come along and spoil it. Or—when someone doesn't arrive on time, or something doesn't happen on schedule—you immediately think the worst-case scenario. Or maybe there's *always* some fear and worry lurking in the back of your mind. Whatever the case, think of the thousands of times your worrying has proven unwarranted. The overwhelming odds are, this time will have a happy ending, too. Relax, enjoy your life, and for crying out loud, stop worrying. Why make yourself crazy?

309
Don't always feel you have
to be doing something.

We are not human *doings*...we are human *beings*. There's nothing wrong with doing nothing. In fact, it wouldn't hurt to set aside time each day to do just that. *Nothing.* Sit and relax. Or take a stroll. Block out all the clutter in your mind. And then let it wander. At first, you may become anxious thinking of it as downtime—wasted moments when you could be accomplishing something. But guess what? You *are* accomplishing something. You're grabbing the reins of a runaway team of horses and pulling them back into an easy, manageable pace. You're freeing up your mind. Getting control of yourself. Learning that living is not just doing...but being. Cut yourself some slack now and then and carve out some good, healthy nothing time. Why make yourself crazy?

310
Keep the menu simple.

When entertaining there's no need to overwhelm your guests with more choices than necessary. (Why make *them* crazy?). An hors d' oeuvre, a main dish, a couple of side dishes, and dessert is plenty. It will save you time and money, and make entertaining easy enough that you'll want to do it more often. Overdoing it also unfairly raises the stakes for guests who want to reciprocate. Focus on the quality of what you serve, not the quantity, and on making your visitors feel comfortable and welcome. Your get-togethers can't help but turn out special. Why make yourself crazy?

311
Don't buy what you already have.

This may sound obvious, but there are probably several duplicated items in your home right now...*and you don't even know it.* Especially if you tend to accumulate a lot of clutter (see #2 on how to get rid of it). So before you go shopping, check to see that you don't already have what you think you need (the rear of the refrigerator, cabinets and closets are good places to start). Make a list of infrequently used possessions and where they're kept. Over time, you can save a lot of money just by keeping track of what you've already got. Why make yourself crazy?

312
Work close to where you live.

Or live close to where you work. Even work out of your home, if feasible. You might make more money schlepping a distance, but in the long run, is the extra pay worth the lost time with your family, the high commutation expenses and the wear and tear on you? Probably not even close. Get a job near your house. Simplify your lifestyle. Be home for dinner. Watch your kids grow up. Why make yourself crazy?

313
Improve your vocabulary.

It's frustrating not knowing what a word means, thinking it means something else or having to ask people to explain it. If you don't know the definition of something, look it up. Strive each day to learn a new word, how to pronounce it and how to use it. Adding to your vocabulary helps you grasp immediately what the world is communicating, rather than grope around for meaning and clarification. Why make yourself crazy?

314
Call in your kids' restaurant orders before you arrive.

If you have small, antsy, unruly, or especially hungry children (or, God forbid, all of the above), call in your order before you leave for the restaurant. By the time you get there, are seated and settled, the food will soon arrive to grab and hold their attention. Trying to keep young kids entertained and in their chairs is a task. So call ahead, cut the wait and maybe you can even enjoy the experience. Why make yourself crazy?

315
Get all the facts first.

Don't be so quick to judge, accuse or jump to conclusions before all the facts are in. It can hurt others, and it can hurt you. Get the full story—all sides of it—from reliable sources before you pass judgment. Society has developed a lynch-mob mentality, ready to pounce on anyone or anything the minute a rumor takes hold, and is sadly unrepentant when proven wrong. Don't you be a part of it. Get the facts before you act. Why make yourself crazy?

316
Do things off-peak.

Unless you love crowds, jostling and waiting in line, try to get things done when everyone else isn't. Go to the bank, cleaners, supermarket and pharmacy during slow periods. Eat at restaurants later or earlier than the hoi poloi. (You might even be rewarded with an early-bird special.) Vacation during fringe seasons when it's less crowded and a lot cheaper. (Pulling younger kids out of school shouldn't hurt them, especially if you work educational activities into the vacation.) In other words, live conveniently and affordably off-peak. Why make yourself crazy?

317
Don't forget to breathe.

This is one of the most immediate and effective tools for reducing everyday stress. *Yet we rarely use it.* In fact, when tense and pressured, we often do the exact opposite! That's because our natural fight or flight response to stress is shallow, rapid breathing and tensed muscles, preparing us to either fight or flee. But since we rarely do that anymore (hopefully), we have to consciously override our default response and remember to take a slow, deep, lung-filling breath or two every so often, especially during ticklish and trying moments of the day—hundreds of times if need be. Claim the air you need to succeed. Why make yourself crazy?

318
Don't try to replicate past events.

They'll rarely be as good as the first time around, and more likely disappointing. Instead, strive for fresh experiences that in themselves will one day become poignant memories. Why try to recapture the past when you already have it? Why make yourself crazy?

319
Sleep on it.

Time and your subconscious are excellent decision makers, editors, problem solvers, and healers. So when it's late, and you're tired and perplexed, simply go to bed. Let your mind do the work while you're enjoying a good night's sleep. Chances are, you'll awaken to a better answer, a brighter outlook, a clearer understanding of what to do. Why make yourself crazy?

320
Bored? Shake up your routine.

Your day doesn't always have to follow the same lackluster script. Break out of your jaded routine and experience life in fresh new ways. Maybe it's eating breakfast out, taking a different route to work, reading a section of the newspaper you never do, visiting a store or attraction you normally pass by, revamping your style of dress, modifying the way you treat or interact with others. Each is nothing earth-shattering in itself, but it affirms the power you have to make things happen, to change your perspective, to inject excitement and diversity into everything you do. Break the rigid, monotonous regimens of your life. Why make yourself crazy?

321
Learn to listen.

Don't merely pay ear service...carefully *listen* to what people are saying to you. Make a conscious effort to hear and understand every word they speak. Resist the urge to interrupt, and wait till the speaker has finished completely before responding. Don't miss key parts of the message because you're thinking of something else, or prematurely forming your response. And be sensitive to implied or hidden meanings behind the words—that is, what the speaker is really trying to communicate. You'll be amazed at how much more you'll learn and understand when you truly listen. Why make yourself crazy?

322
Be persistent.

Don't be put off, shunted aside, delayed, or denied because someone else doesn't want to do his job, or fulfill her obligation, or perform their responsibility. Be persistent, stand your ground and get what you're entitled to. Refuse to accept partial, less-than-adequate or vague responses to things you have a right to know, or services you're paying for. Sometimes it's easier and less confrontational to give in, but that only leads to anger, stress and frustration. And encourages people to take advantage of you, and those who follow you. Keep them honest; demand satisfaction. Why make yourself crazy?

323
Get off the upgrade treadmill.

Products like computers, software, TVs, cars, skis, and stereos don't change as fast and dramatically as their makers would like you to think. They'll pull out the stops to convince you that what you have now is passé or obsolete (even though they recently sold it to you!). Don't buy it. If the item serves your main purpose, and serves it well, keep it. A few more bells and whistles, or a marginal increase in performance, isn't worth the extra expense and hassle. Why make yourself crazy?

324
Store things out of the way.

Take an extra moment or two to put things back where they belong. Why? Because you can bet that wherever you put them temporarily, they will soon be annoyingly in the way. So you end up moving the item two or three times, when you only had to do it once. More than that, things left out tend to reproduce (I swear they do) and multiply to the point where work surfaces and living space soon disappear. Nip those stragglers in the bud and haul them out of sight. Why make yourself crazy?

325
Create a mudroom.

Or a mud area. A transition place where weathered footwear and outer garments can be shed, along with the day's travails and concerns. A comfortable space where you can warm up or cool down, and avoid tracking in unwanted dirt and moisture. A mud area will keep your home cleaner and more orderly, while leaving just one small space to tidy up. Why make yourself crazy?

326
Recognize when you've attained "enough."

One of the weaknesses of our culture is not stopping, or even knowing, when we've achieved enough. Which leads to excess, exhaustion, egotism, insatiable appetites, and damaged relationships. Learn the point at which you've worked enough, rested enough, spoken enough, eaten enough, drunk enough, exercised enough, complained enough, and beaten your opponent enough. Know when you've accumulated enough possessions, taken on enough debt, received enough praise. In recognizing these limits, you can eliminate the lack of fulfillment and sense of futility we feel when we can never achieve "enough." Why make yourself crazy?

327
Confirm your appointments.

Will your friend remember your lunch date? Will your flight take off on schedule? Will the repairperson you've taken a day off from work to let in, show up? Don't leave yourself guessing. Or, worse, empty-handed. A one-minute phone call to confirm the event can save you a lot of grief and hassle later on. Why make yourself crazy?

328
Research your purchases.

Get objective reviews of products and services from consumer magazines, Internet sites, message boards, friends, and relatives whose opinions you respect. You'll soon get a valid consensus of which products are right for you, and which to avoid. And don't use a lack of time as an excuse for not doing re-search. You'll spend a lot more of it, and money too, if you have to replace an item that turns out to be a dog. Get it right the first time. Do the legwork. Why make yourself crazy?

329
Don't forget the little projects.

In our efforts to concentrate on the big kahunas of our life—work, school, family, relationships—we often forget to service the smaller needs: minor repairs and upkeep, organizing cluttered living spaces, catching up on paperwork...in general the everyday mainte-nance of our lives. Overlooked, these things can pile up, get in your face, detract from your quality of life. Actually, these lesser projects can offer you refreshing breaks from major pursuits. And keeping pace with them will impart a sense of order and satisfaction, that things are under control. So take care of the little stuff, too. Why make yourself crazy?

330
Always have a trip planned.

Whether it's a weekend jaunt or a world tour, the mere act of planning a future vacation is liberating, uplifting and exciting to look forward to. And you don't even have to spend money to start the process. Read up on places you'd like to go, send away for brochures, block out the time, and begin enjoying the wonderful benefits that travel offers...before, during and after. Always have an escape planned. Why make yourself crazy?

331
Don't use your busyness to justify bad habits.

How convenient. You're so busy you don't have time to exercise! Or get enough sleep. Or eat a nutritious meal. It'll just have to be cheeseburgers and fries again. Do you find yourself doing this? Using your overloaded schedule—indeed even beefing it up—as a way to avoid doing things you know you should...but don't want to make the effort? Be honest here. There's no excuse for not taking time to take proper care of yourself. *Your health and fitness should always come first.* When they do, when you make them top priority, you'll not only be better able to manage a busy schedule and its attendant stress. You'll have the strength of mind not to commit to excessive activities that jeopardize your well-being in the first place. Bottom line: be careful not to hide behind your stressful lifestyle. Why make yourself crazy?

332
The stress of terror.

As if you don't already have enough to worry about, you have to contend with the knowledge there are people out there plotting to kill you. Or destroy your way of life. If it's any consolation, this is nothing new in the history of mankind. There always was, always will be those who want to impose their beliefs on others, dominate them, even randomly kill them. The difference today is the violence of the methods used and the global media attention each episode receives. While you can't ignore this reality, neither should you live your life in terror. Go about your days with cautious awareness, savoring each one that passes in safety and freedom. And, in whatever way you can, support efforts not only to root out terrorists and prevent their deadly acts, but promote the kind of cooperation and understanding among people that deters hatred in the first place. Why make yourself crazy?

333
Write it down immediately.

Before you forget, jot down the name of that restaurant, the person you're supposed to call, the time of the next practice, the great website you heard about... whatever useful information has just been given you.

Chances are, with everything else cramming your brain, you'll otherwise forget it. That's why a PDA (personal digital assistant) is always a good thing to have handy. Don't miss out. Write it down. Why make yourself crazy?

334
Do you stress when it comes to tipping?

Few things are as cloaked in ambiguity and awkwardness as the common gratuity. Whether or not to tip, whom to tip, when to tip, and how much to tip are perplexing questions. And in an increasingly service-oriented society, more and more tipping situations present more occasions to squirm. Some general guidelines. When in doubt, tip. Or at least offer a tip. It's a lot better than not tipping and later agonizing over it. If you're afraid you might insult the person, simply ask "Do you accept gratuities?" as you present the tip. They've no doubt been through this before and won't be as fazed about it as you are. Of course, if the service is lousy or the provider rude, feel no compunction about stiffing them. How much to tip? That depends on a lot of things, but you can find help at: http://azaz.essortment.com/tipping_rdef.htm and other web sites. Why make yourself crazy?

335
Whenever you're feeling the stressed-out victim...

Think of some really dumb or reckless thing you did in your past that thank heaven didn't turn out to be the disaster it could have been. Now use that gratitude and relief to put whatever stress you're currently experiencing into perspective. In fact, the mere thought of the breaks you caught in life should loosen you up, make you feel like you're playing with the house's money, lucky even to have the chance to be doing what you're doing. So summon up the liberating feeling of those narrow escapes whenever you're feeling victimized. Things could be a heck of a lot worse. Why make yourself crazy?

336
Live for today with an eye toward tomorrow.

With so much emphasis on gearing up for the future, you may be missing out on the present! And these are perhaps the best years of your life. Why get so caught up in how great things are *going* to be, you all but ignore the wonderful gifts you have now? Among them: youth, health, children, family, friendships, peace, opportunity. You don't have to attain a certain income level or social status as a qualification to enjoy life. And it's foolish to devote all your energies—indeed knock yourself out—on rewards you'll realize only at a distant time (if at all). Granted, you have to move in a general direction that ensures a secure future. But your main focus should be on the here and now. This is your life. It's precious. So make every moment of it count. Why make yourself crazy?

337
Visualize.

Picturing in your mind beforehand how you want something to turn out can strongly influence how it actually does. At the very least it will positively affect your approach to it. So do a mental run-through of the event first. For example, visualize yourself as an enthusiastic contributor at a business meeting. See yourself hitting a golf ball successfully before taking a swing. Picture a calm, harmonious evening with the family. (Yes, it's possible!) While it won't assure you'll get the desired result, it will certainly help. Conversely, negative visualization can adversely affect a situation. So try to avoid it. (Remember, things usually aren't as bad as we imagine they'll be.) When you visualize the way you'd like something ideally to play out, you're already one step closer to achieving it. Why make yourself crazy?

338
Are you uncomfortable with calmness?

As hard as it is to get rid of stress, when we finally do, it sometimes makes us uneasy! Why? Because many see a composed person as unambitious, slacking off, apathetic. If you aren't hyped up and frazzled, you couldn't possibly be doing a good job. So you feel pressure to look busy and overwhelmed. That's how twisted our society's thinking has become. Don't give in to it. Stick to your stress-free demeanor. When they see how efficient and productive you are, it'll dawn on them there's a better way. And you can remain comfortable in your calm proficiency. Why make yourself crazy?

339
Things to chuckle over, rather than stress over.

You try to start your car while the engine is running. Your straw slips irretrievably into the soda bottle. Your movie seat lists to starboard. Your voice suddenly breaks into falsetto. The chocolate coating on your ice cream pop slides off onto your hand. A flying cicada crashes into your head. Something falls under the bed and you just...can't...reach...it. You get a shopping cart with one wheel that won't move. You've got this one song in your head and it's driving you nuts. Life is filled with these kinds of everyday aggravations. Learn to laugh at them. Why make yourself crazy?

340
Kick the sugar habit.

With each new study that comes out, the case against eating too much refined sugar (which also includes corn syrup, fructose and honey) grows ever stronger. Do a Google search of "dangers of sugar" to gain a more balanced perspective on this, given the billions of dollars spent yearly urging you to consume soft drinks, cakes, cookies, ice cream, snacks, and other foods loaded with sugar. You might be shocked at the numerous conditions attributed to the sweet stuff. From a stress standpoint alone, if you experience periods of unexplained anxiousness during the day, a roller coaster ride of highs and lows, occasional jitters, or even panic attacks...try cutting your intake of refined sugar for a couple of weeks. (Eat fresh fruit instead.) If you start feeling steadier, less anxious, more confident, and healthier overall...you've hit it on the nose. Why make yourself crazy?

341
Boil your children's choices down to either/or.

Getting your kids involved in decision-making is a good thing. It teaches them responsibility, builds confidence and self-reliance. But giving them *too* many choices can be confusing, stressful and overwhelming. (Just as it is for adults!) So simplify their selection process. Examples: "Would you like to go to the park today? Or do a craft?" "Do you want to wear your blue shirt, or the yellow?" Also, couching an unwanted prospect in a choice can make it more palatable: "It's time for bed. Would you like me to read this story...or that one?" Uncomplicated either/or decisions. They'll make your child's life easier. They'll make your life easier. Why make yourself crazy?

342
Relax to the aroma of home cooking.

This is something you simply don't get with meals that are microwaved, boiled in a bag, or scooped out of a can. Home-cooked items like oven roasts, sautéed onions, baked bread, grilled fish, simmering sauces,

and stir-fry do more than provide a wholesomely delicious meal. They fill the air with comforting, stress-
reducing aromas that will ease the tensions and lift
the spirits of the entire household. Your lifestyle may
be ultra-convenient, but lacking in the olfactory sensa-
tions that evoke warm feelings and reassuring
thoughts. It'll do you well to get in the kitchen and put
together a good old-fashioned home cooked meal. Why
make yourself crazy?

343
Alternate mental and physical activities.

If you work at a desk all day, don't sit in front of
the TV all night. Do something active. If your job is
physical, or involves being on your feet or running
around, relax and exercise your mind (like reading a
book) during the off hours. If your work involves both
mental and physical aspects, try alternating the two
throughout the day. What this does is add balance
and vitality to your life. It's more energizing, stress-
reducing and healthier overall. It's easy to get stuck
in a single monotonous mode—like moving from chair
to chair all day—and suppress your other self. It's essential to exercise both your mind and body. Why
make yourself crazy?

344
Build in the expectation
of malfunctions.

When we buy things—homes, cars, appliances, computers—in our enthrallment with their newness and pride of acquisition, we never imagine them breaking down, needing repair, or eventually being replaced. So when it actually happens, it comes as a shock to us, a stroke of misfortune we didn't deserve. Causing much anxiety and stress. Look, these aren't anomalies, they're normal occurrences. Each year, expect that some items will break and need fixing or replacement. You just don't know what they'll be. Also, set aside a certain dollar amount, at least in your mind, you can expect to pay. Then, when something goes kaput, you won't feel victimized. And will treat it like the routine event it is. Why make yourself crazy?

345
Expect it to take longer
and cost more.

Whatever it is—a home improvement, a new appliance, a vacation, a repair, a recipe—it's our human nature to underestimate how long it will take and how much it will cost. So rather than set yourself up for a nasty surprise, start high, think worst case scenario, and fully expect it to be more than you initially thought it would be. And if for some incredible reason it isn't, it's like getting a bonus. Hope for the best but don't count on it. Why make yourself crazy?

346
Eat slowly.

A meal is a gift, a source of pleasure, a time to re-lax and replenish. So why diminish the experience by scarfing it down like it may be your last? This may take some doing, but get into the habit of eating slowly. Chew deliberately and savor each bite. Take frequent pauses. Give your body a chance to accept and digest the food, rather than shocking and over-whelming it. And try not to think about finishing fast so you can get to something else. *This* is what you want to be doing. So give each repast the enjoyment and sociality it deserves. Why make yourself crazy?

347
Be careful whom you confide in.

Sometimes it's less risky to divulge your personal problems to a stranger on an airplane than a friend or coworker. If you doubt this, look at all the kiss-and-tell books out there where someone publicly bashes for their own gain another person they're supposed to love. Today, even your most trusted confidants might someday turn on you and use your innermost secrets to their political or monetary advantage. It's an unfortunate failing of our culture, but one to take seriously. Sure, you'll still find people whose loyalty is unflinching. But if you have any inkling of doubt about another's character or sincerity, no matter how chummy things are now, it's best to keep your personal issues close to the vest. Why make yourself crazy?

348
Go biking.

Biking is healthy. Biking is fun. You can do it at any age, at whatever intensity you wish. You can bike to run errands, visit others, enjoy an outing with the family, or just get some needed exercise and a refreshing break. You can also rent bikes when you travel. It's a great way to sightsee and explore. All of which contributes measurably to relieving stress in your life. To get set up with the right bike, and learn more about the health benefits of cycling and biking safety, do an Internet search. There are loads of sites out there that can help you. If you've been seeking an active alternative to your pressured routine, biking may be it. Why make yourself crazy?

349
Parenting shouldn't be a guilt trip.

How we agonize over the raising of our kids! Are we firm enough? Too strict? Are we providing them with everything they need? Or spoiling them? Why do we always feel we can be doing a better job...we don't spend enough time with them...we're neglecting their needs? Regardless of how hard we're trying! And then, we have to compete with the Dad who gets his son into the pro team's locker room, and the Mom who hires a recording star to entertain at her daughter's birthday. Forget all that. Give them love, give them limits, listen to what they have to say, and instill in them—through your own example—a set of good moral values. Do that, and you'll never have cause to feel like an unworthy parent. Why make yourself crazy?

350
Tired of giving out information?

The constant quest by others for information about you can be maddening. You're forever filling out forms, applications, coupons, registrations, reply cards. You get badgered on the telephone to participate in surveys. You're hit up for your name and email address to enter websites. Store cashiers presumptuously ask for your phone number or zip code. And you're weary of answering questions about your job at social gatherings. Everybody wants to know who you are, where you live, what you do, and how many times a week you floss. And in the majority of cases it's none of their business. So in the interest of protecting your time, your privacy and your sanity, don't give out any information to people and organizations who have their nose where it doesn't belong. Why make yourself crazy?

351
More things to chuckle over, rather than stress over.

The locker room bench is just the right width so that everything you put on it falls off. You mistakenly dial a fax line and get an ear-piercing beep for your trouble. You can't separate the shopping cart from the pack. Horseflies are ingenious at getting into your house, but can never get out. Your spouse serves for dinner the same thing you had for lunch. Every time you use an airplane bathroom you hit turbulence. You go out to select wallpaper, thinking you'll be back in an hour. You're clueless how to dispose of the pizza box. The paint that barely covers the wall takes forever to wash out of the brush. That's life. Laugh at it. Why make yourself crazy?

352
Open the closed doors of your life.

A closed door is: *I can't do that. That's not me. I'm too old. It's too late. I'm too busy. I don't know enough about it. They won't take me seriously.* Nonsense. Remove these artificial barriers to greater joy and accomplishment. Cross the threshold to enriching new experience. Make the investment in time and effort to rise above the dull routine of your life to develop new talents, new friendships and strike out in new directions. The only real obstacle is you. Recognize this. Just open the door (there are no locks) and walk through. Why make yourself crazy?

353
Leave personal politics
out of the office.

Talk to a man for half an hour and he will more than likely incautiously reveal his political leanings. Women generally are more discreet in this regard. While it might be reassuring to find people at work who share your political views, it's a good bet others don't. And proclaiming your beliefs too righteously, frequently or vociferously can create tension and stress around you. Even provoke ridicule. There's also the possibility that those in authority will take umbrage at your decided opinions. Be open to diverse points of view and sensitive to offending others or making them uncomfortable. In the same way another's impassioned rants might make you feel. As a rule, it's best to your keep personal politics out of the workplace. Why make yourself crazy?

354
Every moment is an opportunity.

Do you find yourself forever waiting for opportunities to happen? And thus are stuck in a frustrating holding pattern until they do? It might surprise you that every moment of your life is an opportunity. Everything you think, everything you say and do is the result of a decision you make. And you have the opportunity to make each of those decisions different, exciting, better. The reason life becomes so monotonous and predictable is that we're constantly making the same decisions. We don't fully explore our options. Start changing that. See how differently you can meet each moment. The affect can be startling, empowering, liberating. And the more you take advantage of these opportunities, the more they will make themselves apparent to you. Why make yourself crazy?

355
Take it to the next level.

When something goes wrong, try to avoid getting mired in the usual reactions of anger, frustration, disappointment and despair. Instead, hoist yourself to another level—one of understanding, acceptance and fortitude. Say to yourself: *Yes, this is tough, but if I can meet the challenge and get through it—and I will—not only will I have dealt with this problem, but I will be that much stronger to tackle an even worse crisis should one come along.* Sure, it's not easy. But if you ratchet up your reaction to strife a notch or two, and meet it head on, you'll emerge in much better shape. Why make yourself crazy?

356
Where have all the heroes gone?

On a recent radio talk show, hosts and callers were at a loss to name anyone today who could truly be called a hero—that is, a selfless individual who has contributed to society in a courageous and significant way, and could be looked up to and emulated. Everyone mentioned had a major disqualifying flaw or was mired in self-interest. So where have all the heroes gone? They haven't gone anywhere. Society simply chooses to ignore the achievements of decent, honest people...and instead worships at the altars of steroid-juiced athletes, greed-driven business leaders and venal politicians. The real hero may be the guy sitting next to you. The person you're married to. Maybe even you! So don't fall into the trap of following the lead of corrupt, self-absorbed icons. Just look around you. There are heroes all over the place. Why make yourself crazy?

357
Don't be so dismissive.

Do you often summarily reject something or find an excuse to deem it unworthy, not because it lacks merit, but simply out of expediency? Because you're too busy to properly evaluate it? Be careful. At such times it's very easy to pass over an extraordinary opportunity. (Note the word "miss" in dismissive.) Ideally, you should never let yourself become so overwhelmed you cut yourself off from exploring new ideas and directions. Even in a frazzled state, you should never reject something or someone outright before giving them at least a cursory investigation. It could be the very thing that springs you from the indentured life of stress you're living. Why make yourself crazy?

358
Don't let others waste your time.

Some people have no stress empathy. They see that you're totally crazed (or do they?), yet needlessly interrupt you, get in your way, engage you in small talk, and otherwise make a nuisance of themselves. These are often people you work with, or are close to, and don't want to offend. Be polite, be diplomatic, but firmly convey the message you're way too busy to schmooze. Seek commiseration: "You won't believe how swamped I am." Or look at your watch and exclaim: "Yikes! You'll have to excuse me..." If these don't work, simply ask them to give you a hand. That's right. Ask for help. It will usually get rid of them, or even better, they just might pitch in. In any case, use your ingenuity and always have a good evasive tactic at the ready. Why make yourself crazy?

359
Get organized.

This is for all you Oscar Madisons out there, whose daily lives are in a constant state of disarray—often characterized by messiness, lateness, losing things, forgetting things, and being otherwise unorganized. The biggest obstacle to getting things under control is knowing where to start. The short answer is: *any-*

where. It doesn't matter. It could be a major household clean-up or the simple purging of your address book. But once you've broken into the cycle, don't stop. Keep the momentum going and let it spread to each area of your life—both the physical and the mental. There are books and resources galore to help you through each phase. Disorganization can be a monumental waste of your talents and energy. Don't let it happen. Get serious and get it together. Why make yourself crazy?

360
Don't be *over*-organized.

This one is for all of you Felix Ungers. There's such a thing as being *too* organized. And it can be just as stressful as being disorganized. It's when you've got your nose so involved in details and plans, you're often unaware of what's actually going on. Over-organizers are so rigid and regimented, they can't adjust to changing situations or think on the fly. People skills suffer, too, since the constant fretting and fussing rub many the wrong way. Realize that a plan is just that, an outline, and that real action, real people, are what matter most. (We don't go to the movies to read scripts.) So come up with your plan, then let go and let things happen. Be human, be flexible, be understanding. And all will turn out fine. Why make yourself crazy?

361
When things start to unravel...

Ask yourself this question: Am I making myself crazy? Just the fact that you have to ask it means you probably are. And if the answer is yes, there's likely a strategy you've learned in this book, or one you can devise yourself, that will help you deal with the situation. Know the point at which it's time to ask that critical question, so you can call a timeout and avert a far worse scenario from developing. Gaining that sixth sense takes practice, but once conditioned to asking yourself "Am I making myself crazy?" you can avoid virtually every potentially stressful issue you face. Why make yourself crazy?

362
When you hit an obstacle,
go around it.

Not through it. Not over it. Around it. You'll find that most of life's travails can be deftly circumvented rather than toughed out. Avoided instead of confronted. You may think that's a copout, a sign of a weak character. On the contrary. It's smart. How do you think those in power and authority stay that way? By sidestepping the sucker punches. By choosing their fights judiciously. And infrequently. The reality is, we can ill afford to exhaust our energies rising to meet every challenge that's thrown at us. It's a sure recipe for becoming a burned-out walking zombie. Don't always feel you have to battle it out on the high road. Know when to seek the path of least resistance. Why make yourself crazy?

363
Don't compromise your principles at work.

What we're pressured to do in our jobs sometimes conflicts with our personal values. We succumb to the corporate mentality that if everyone else in the company is doing it, it must be okay. Or we aren't given a choice. That's why organizations with basically good people sometimes do awful things. These are not easy situations to extricate yourself from, especially when your livelihood depends on it. But the guilt and stress that builds over time can eat away at you physically and damage your self-worth. Try to be a force for change within your organization. Barring that, you might have to bail out altogether. Either way, stick to your moral convictions. Why make yourself crazy?

364
The best defense is a good offense.

A good way to get demanding people off your back is to get on theirs. For example, if someone at work is always bugging you for things they can just as easily get for themselves (assuming it's not your boss), go on the offensive. Start hitting *them* up with requests. The last thing they want is to do for others what they're too lazy to do for themselves. They'll quietly vanish. The same with freeloaders. Got a neighbor who keeps asking for favors yet never reciprocates? Show up at their door a few times to borrow something. They'll avoid you like the plague. Enjoy the just payback that goes with this. It's very empowering to turn the tables on someone who uses you...and watch them turn tail and run. Why make yourself crazy?

365
Set up a stress relief fund.

Put aside some money, about $50 to $100, and sock it away somewhere in your house where it will be available at a moment's notice. This is not vacation money, not typical fun money and should not be used capriciously. But when things really start cranking up and you're all but fried...break into your emergency stress fund. Go out and do something totally unplanned and indulgent. Whether it's a favorite restaurant, store, nightclub, sporting event, whatever...is up to you. But when things are getting too insane, declare yourself a disaster area and send in some aid. Why make yourself crazy?

366
Don't put off that difficult phone call.

You know you have to make that call. To appease an unhappy client. To confront another with a serious accusation. To solicit a donation from a skinflint. To ask someone out. To discuss a sensitive issue. To turn someone down. It's not easy to do. But it has to be done. The longer you wait, the harder it gets. And the more the anxiety builds. So take a breath. Bite the bullet. Make the call. You'll feel a whole lot better when it's done. Why make yourself crazy?

367
If someone isn't interested, let it go.

Naturally we want other people to like what we like, to share our interests and concerns, to experience for themselves the joy we find in things. We want our children to partake in the same activities we loved as kids, our friends to marvel at the movie we found so wonderful, others to take up a cause we deem so important. But when they show little interest, or don't even respond, we can't understand it. It distresses us. Why can't they see? Are they ignorant? No. Just different. Look, it's okay to make your case to someone. But leave it at that. You can't will your preferences on others. You tried. They declined. So let it go. Just be grateful you've found what you've found, and hope that they, too, might hit upon something equally significant. Why make yourself crazy?

368
Meltdown? Or brownout?
Take your pick.

There are times when we're so harried and overwhelmed by circumstances we simply lose it. Futility, exasperation, blow-ups, tantrums, and tears often ensue. Things are said, impulsive decisions are made, we may later regret. You should never let it get that far. When symptoms of a pending meltdown appear, do what the electric companies do during periods of high demand. Go into brownout mode. Take your intensity level down a notch or two. Realize you're just one person, there are limits to what you can do, and it's just not possible to be everywhere and solve every problem. Your best will have to suffice. This acceptance will not only be a tremendous relief, it will allow you to carry on without overloading your circuits and shutting down altogether. Blow-up or brownout? Why make yourself crazy?

369
Refuse to be strung along...

Newscasts are notorious for teasing you throughout the entire show with the prospect of a riveting story that turns out to be a dud. Companies lure you in with a low price that's no bargain when all the fine-print fees are tacked on. Politicians...well, they'll tell you anything to get your vote. Don't be a fool for any of these ploys. They're playing with you, toying with your emotions to suck you in. So give them what they deserve. Change the channel, shop elsewhere, vote for the other guy. And don't return. If their come-on is underhanded, you have to assume everything else about them isn't much different. Why make yourself crazy?

370
Don't let one ruin it for all.

Like the loudmouth at the game who spoils the occasion for everyone nearby. The kid in school who disrupts the entire class so no one learns. The neighbor whose neglected property blights the entire block. Moviegoers who won't shut up during the show. Don't let it continue one stressful minute longer than neces-sary. You have options. Use them. Politeness and for-bearance don't come into play when your rights are be-ing stepped on. So seek immediate help from the auth-orities who are responsible for remedying such aggra-vations and restore things for the good of all. Why make yourself crazy?

371
Is stress making you a klutz?

Stress can render us about as graceful as the Three Stooges. In your careless haste, do you some-times bash your shin on the corner of the coffee ta-ble...fling your cell phone out of your pocket and onto the street...try to get out of your car with the seatbelt on...knock your coffee all over the desk...miss the last step? Blame it on stress. It makes bungling fools of us all. Being in a frenzy should be an early tip-off that you're very likely to do something klutzy. So take ex-tra care at such times. You don't want to make a bad situation worse. Why make yourself crazy?

372
You can't say it. But you can *think* it!

It's frustrating when your position or political cor-rectness force you to bite your tongue or sweeten your words when you'd much prefer to tell someone off in no uncertain terms. But there's nothing preventing you from expressing your true feelings internally. For example, you might say to your boss, "Sure, I can do that," while adding in your mind *"but it's a really stupid idea."* Or you ask the sales clerk "Can I get some help here?" while thinking *"Stop yakking and do your job!"* Cheeky internal dialogue is an effective way to release tension and even lighten a stressful situation by injecting some irreverent humor into your thoughts. (Just don't forget yourself and blurt it out loud.) Why make yourself crazy?

373
You've got enough stress.
Don't go asking for it.

It's one thing to be faced with a stressful situation that's uninvited. But don't go setting yourself up for one. Like saying to your guests: "Take your time, whenever you get here is fine." Bad idea. They'll keep you waiting for hours. Be specific. Set a time. Or agreeing to terms you *don't* agree with out of politeness—like taking less compensation. Politely *dis*agree. Or saying "that's okay" when someone abuses your kindness or generosity. It's *not* okay. And they should know it. Don't be a shock absorber for the inconsiderateness of others.

There's only so much stress you can take. Why make yourself crazy?

374
You don't have to associate with people you don't like.

You may find some individuals distasteful, egotistical, rude, selfish, condescending, unprincipled, raunchy, rowdy, or just plain creepy. Or maybe you can't explain why you don't like someone...you just don't. It stresses you just to be in their presence. When you are, treat them with the same kindness and respect you'd afford anyone else. Then quickly move on. If you can avoid them altogether, so much the better. There's no rule, law or moral precept that says you have to socialize or do business with everyone. (Love thy neighbor doesn't mean you have to *like* them.) There are enough positive, upbeat people to surround yourself with, without having to consort with those who bum you out. Why make yourself crazy?

375
Take advantage of the cooling off period.

This is a very effective tool when you're angry at someone or something (and how often is that!) and prone to react in ways that aggravate the situation rather than defuse it. Next time you're incensed, allow yourself a chunk of time to cool off. A good start is to write down exactly what you *might* have done, or said, at the height of your fury. This in itself will help dissipate some of the anger. More importantly, when you read it later on, you'll get a sobering picture of what might have happened had you not declared a cooling off period. And realize how easy it is to overreact. Note that cooling off doesn't mean suppressing your stress so it's still smoldering and festering underneath. It means giving yourself time to vent your inflamed emotions in a more gradual, safer way. Work on keeping your cool. Why make yourself crazy?

376
Get a yearly physical...religiously.

Don't keep putting it off. You may feel great. You may look great. (*Despite* your stress.) But many ailments don't walk up and tap you on the shoulder. They can progress silently, insidiously, without symptoms. So it's imperative to go for an annual checkup to ensure everything's functioning properly. And detect any trouble early on. The brief anticipation of seeing a doctor pales in comparison to the stress you carry around postponing it. (Especially if you *are* experiencing symptoms.) Or the satisfaction you'll enjoy getting a clean bill of health. Don't be so cavalier about this. Or vaguely remind yourself to remind yourself. Make an appointment *today*. You'll feel better getting it on the calendar. And off your mind. Why make yourself crazy?

377
How long must you endure a bad choice?

Somehow—you don't quite know why, or how—you think you picked the wrong career, school, doctor, business partner, babysitter, contractor, financial advisor, supplier... And it's stressing you to no end. First, be sure you're not just being peevish, impatient, intractable, or one-sided. What may be required is a simple adjustment, compromise or getting-used-to period. Give it at least that. For more serious cases, a face-to-face sit-down or outside advice may be in order. It will cut the tension and bring issues to the surface. But if you've tried to make it work, in earnest—without success—it's time to accept your mistake and move to correct it. The worst thing to do is let it grind on unresolved and suffer increasingly harmful consequences. We all make bad choices. The difference is in how and when we endeavor to address them. Why make yourself crazy?

378
Are you an inveterate deviator?

Not deviate, deviator. That is, one who is so easily and often distracted you become three tasks removed from the one you should be doing. To the point where you completely forget about the first one until you stumble across it later on. Sometimes of course you have no choice. Life can unfold in frantic bursts. But how often do you give in to distractions you know full well aren't important and leave you scurrying to catch up? It can be habit forming—a self-inflicted attention deficit disorder that disrupts your focus and work-flow. The solution is simple. Whenever you're tempted to sidetrack, ask yourself: is this detour worth taking? Then summon the resolve to pass on it. Why make yourself crazy?

379
Spend more one-on-one
time with loved ones.

Due to an overall lack of time, there's a tendency for families to spend most of it together as a group...trying to cover all bases at once. Nothing wrong with that occasionally. But you also need to spend one-on-one time with your children, spouse, parents, and other loved ones individually. There's a different dynamic at work when it's just the two of you. There's no competition for attention. Kids feel more special. And you can better understand each other's needs and address problems. Busy people often fear they're neglecting personal relationships and missing out on the intimacy that everyone needs. So make the effort to stake out periodic one-on-one time. It's important to you, it's important to them. Why make yourself crazy?

380
Don't be small.

Not in a physical sense. But in a way that makes you petty and shortsighted. We all do this to some extent. Dwelling on minor flaws. Constantly judging people. Cracking hurtful jokes at someone else's expense. Being persnickety, peevish, gossipy, or selfishly frugal. The more you give in to these trivialities the smaller you get. Look past them. It's not worth getting mired in trifling circumstances. See the big picture, the overriding purpose, the inherent good in people rather than focusing on insignificant faults. You'll see a marked easing of tension and stress in your own life as you let these things slide. Why make yourself crazy?

381
Don't mistake vacation for life.

You're on vacation. You're in the most pleasant setting. Having the most wonderful time. Everyone is cheerful, friendly, kind. The food is great. Stress is nonexistent. You say to yourself, "I can get used to this." And you think this is the way life should be all the time. And agonize over the improbability of ever achieving that kind of "freedom" and independence. Hold on. It may seem like nirvana now in contrast to your regular doings. But (hard to believe) you'd soon grow sick of it. The point is, you don't have to go to the opposite extreme to live an enriching, stress-free life. Just a modest move toward the middle can have an enormously positive effect. Remember, you still need the good stress: challenges, goals, purpose. It's the constant bad stress that's the culprit. So enjoy your vacation for what it is. A revitalizing temporary break. Why make yourself crazy?

382
Be optimistic...as long as it's *realistic*.

Optimism is great, but if you constantly set your sites much higher than what realistically can be achieved, you may be setting yourself up for frequent disappointment. And that can deflate your optimism over time. By all means live your life optimistically. Just set your goals near enough out there that you can reasonably attain them. That will strengthen and build on your optimism. To the point where you'll become a true optimist—that is, one who can find the positive in anything, regardless of the negative circumstances. Be optimistic. But realistic, too. Why make yourself crazy?

383
Is your cell phone becoming
a stress zone?

Granted, in one respect having a cell phone is a great stress reliever. We can be immediately in touch with those important to us. That's reassuring. But there's a price we pay for instant accessibility. When your cell phone is always on, it's unsettling to know your privacy can be breeched at any moment. It's also disconcerting when it rings at awkward times, or puts you at risk scrambling to answer it. Not to mention intrusive rings and loud conversations in public places that stress everyone. A cell phone comes with its own set of anxieties. So don't let it run your life. Don't give everyone your number and carte blanche to call you at any time. Keep your cell phone turned off unless you're expecting an important call. You can always check your voicemail when convenient. Declare your independence from the phone, rather than let it master *you*. Why make yourself crazy?

384
Can't get it done? Isolate yourself.

If there's an important project you need to get done and your hectic life and constant distractions simply aren't permitting it...go into seclusion. Set aside the time and find a place where no one can disturb you. Then get it done. Some tasks are tricky, time-consuming or require uninterrupted concentration and quiet. And the only way you're going to get that is to lock yourself up in a room, spend a few hours in a library, steal away for the day, or spend a weekend in hiding. Whatever it takes. The isolation will do you good. And the completed project will be a huge burden lifted. Why make yourself crazy?

385
Know what you want.

How much of your life do you spend toiling and stressing over things you *don't* want? Or just think you want? Do you pursue goals just because everyone else does? Do you obsess over acquiring things merely for the chase, or the recognition, and could care less once you've got them? Try to identify the vain and unworthy pursuits that needlessly tax your resources. Peel away the layers of self-delusion to determine what exactly it is you want. Truly want. If you're honest, you may find there are only a handful of things—simple, attainable, nonmaterial—you need to make you happy. Focus your attention on achieving those. Why make yourself crazy?

386
Sometimes you have to slip into low gear.

Everyone occasionally feels wiped out, lazy, lethargic. Hard as you try, you just can't rally yourself to any kind of task. So what happens? You often do nothing at all. And that can leave you behind schedule, headed for a stress crisis. There's another option. Slo-mo. When you just can't rev up to normal operating speed, try starting out very slowly to at least gain some momentum, and continue in that deliberate, cruise-control mode. You'll be more in tune with yourself, meet less resistance and still make progress, albeit gradual. It's similar to the way your body automatically relaxes and slows down when you have a cold. When you're a worn-out hare, it's time to call up the turtle in you. Why make yourself crazy?

387
Inject more of the arts into your life.

Science helps us to live better; art is what we live for. Think how dreary and monotonous our lives would be without books, movies, music, drama, dance, and fine art. And that's exactly what happens when you're overwhelmed and don't create time to enjoy these life-affirming and enriching cultural pursuits. You may think they're dispensable, but without them you can become repressed, angry, one-dimensional. You de-prive yourself of revitalizing breaks from the stressful grind. View the arts not as casual diversions, but es-sential nourishment of the mind and spirit. Why make yourself crazy?

388
Rough day? Latch onto a
plus and don't let go.

Your day is proceeding horribly. You're down, irri-table and feeling defeated. At such times, grab onto something positive, however small, like clutching a passing branch as you're swept along in a raging river. Cling to that, then find another encouraging thought to gain a better foothold, and keep adding to it until you've hoisted yourself back onto safe, con-structive ground. Granted, this often requires great internal strength and resolve, but it's far better than risking what awaits you if you give in to your negative funk and are dragged perilously over the falls. Why make yourself crazy?

389
How much energy do you squander on stress?

Remember, constant everyday stress not only subjects you to undue pressure and anxiety, it wears you out mentally and physically. You only have so much energy each day to expend. And stress can eat up a lot of it. You grow tired more quickly, fizzle out sooner and are forced to rest. It's like getting fewer miles per gallon because you're driving too fast. So why fritter away precious energy on needless stress when you can put it to more productive and enjoyable use? You're cheating yourself! Why make yourself crazy?

390
Have a sanctuary.

Everyone needs a sanctuary. A place you can slip away to, where you feel safe, comfortable and won't be disturbed. Maybe it's as simple as a favorite chair in a quiet nook of your home. But if that isn't possible, find an easily accessible place near where you live you can escape to: a park, library, church, club, beach, indoor public plaza... Use it frequently. And don't feel obligated to do anything other than rest, unwind, let your mind drift. This is the anti-stress. Why make yourself crazy?

391
Put the holidays back into focus.

At the height of the holiday season, when your stress level is peaking, you're totally crazed, blowing through money, wondering if you're missing the point entirely...do this. Give a gift to someone you don't even know. Maybe it's a child or family you read about in the local paper who's undergoing a severe hardship. Maybe it's a charity gift drive for the down and forgotten. Make the effort to go out and shop for that present. As you're doing so, perhaps concerned about the time and money you're spending, imagine the person on the other end opening it, who has to celebrate their Christmas in this way. Who may not be getting any other gift but yours. Or none at all, if you weren't doing this. Compare that with the Christmas you and your family will enjoy. It's a sobering thought. Let it influence your generosity. Let it temper your excesses. Why make yourself crazy?

392
Learn how to say "no."

If you're a person conditioned to saying "yes" all your life, you probably find it very difficult to say "no." And that inevitably leads to a lot of unnecessary stress. So it's imperative you learn this essential skill. First, don't be wishy-washy or apologetic about it. You haven't done anything wrong, and you certainly shouldn't feel guilty about not doing something you can't, don't want to or will hinder yourself if you do. So be direct, firm: "No, I can't." "No, not this time." "Nope. It's not possible." "No, I'm not interested." Or simply, "no." And leave it at that. You don't owe an explanation. And guess what? People will respect that more than an indecisive, roundabout attempt at a refusal, or a "maybe," which they'll conveniently interpret as a yes. Starting today, practice. Find an opportunity to say no. And do it. Without reservation. Without frills. Without insecurity. Why make yourself crazy?

393
Light up your life.

People, like plants, need light to thrive. For some, a lack of it during the duskier winter months can lead to SAD, Seasonal Affective Disorder, a form of depression. If you think you've got it, get professional help.

But light has benefits for all of us. A properly lit work area will let you see things clearly, helping you work more quickly and efficiently. Strategic use of lighting can brighten your outlook, create a warm and cozy home environment, make you feel safer and less stressed at night. And nothing beats cheerful sunshine and fresh air when you've been cooped up for hours. Make sure you let ample light into your life. Why make yourself crazy?

394
Wear clothes that make you feel good.

Especially when you *don't* feel good. Many people squirrel away their favorite clothes for just the right moment...and hardly ever wear them at all! Do the opposite. Wear the things that make you feel happiest first. And wear them often. They're not doing you any good in the closet. So enjoy the positive vibes and confidence they give you. And bear in mind: the kind of clothes you wear does influence your mood and stress level. So if you want to feel calm, relaxed and tension-free...wear casual, comfortable clothes. If you want to feel bright and cheerful, choose such apparel. Master the art of positive wardrobe selection. Dress to de-stress. Why make yourself crazy?

395
Your mood reflects back on you.

More than you know, your temperament affects your family, coworkers, anyone who comes into contact with you. So if you're stressed, tense, angry, or irritable, don't think it's not sending out negative vibes all around you. Or that it won't come biting back at you in ways that will aggravate your mood even more. In the same way, a positive frame of mind can lift the spirits of those it touches. So be aware of the "weather" you bring along with you. Are you helping to make the atmosphere bright and sunny, or damp and gloomy? Why make yourself—and others—crazy?

396
Don't overbuy perishable foods.

If you end up disposing of a quarter to a third of everything in your refrigerator because it spoils before you eat it, you're more than throwing away good money and good food. Think of the constant pressure you put on yourself and your family to consume it all. You end up either eating more than you want, or feeling guilty at having to toss it. If this is the case, it's time to rethink your shopping habits. Don't buy more perishable food than you're certain you'll run out of...before it perishes. Or leave yourself with too many leftovers that are doomed to be left untouched. (Especially those exiled to the back of the fridge.) Sure, an overflowing basket of fruit might look great on the kitchen counter, but someone's got to eat all that stuff. Why make yourself crazy?

397
Don't over-think it.

While thinking something through before acting is a valuable stress-reducing strategy that's certainly advocated here...you can *overdo* it. Examples would be: getting so caught up in the details you miss the big picture; letting complex theory get in the way of practical reality; internally debating pros and cons to the degree you become immobilized; adhering so stubbornly to preconceived notions you stifle creativity; or simply taking so long to mull it over you blow an opportunity altogether. As wonderful a tool as your mind is, recognize when the time for useful deliberation is over and the moment to act is at hand. Why make yourself crazy?

398
It's never too late.

It's never to late to start out on a totally new path in life...mend a rift in a relationship...right a wrong...

rekindle an old friendship...break a bad habit...get that car you always dreamed about... relocate... forgive someone...reclaim your faith...buy flowers for your loved one...heal old wounds...begin a dialogue...change your mind...get into shape...take up a new hobby... make good on an outstanding debt...or start arriving on time. Life hasn't passed you by. It's out there waiting for you. Experience the revitalizing joy of realizing it wasn't too late after all. Why make yourself crazy?

399
Repeat as directed.

To become physically fit, you don't just exercise for a few days then stop. You have to keep at it and make it a part of your life. It's the same with stress. As stress-free as these strategies can help you become, the outside pressures will always be there, the tendencies to lapse back into stressful habits will continue to dog you. Just because you have a stress-free day today doesn't mean you'll have one tomorrow. That's why it's important to frequently review these daily strategies, remind yourself to implement them and reinforce your resolve. If do that, over time you really *can* make these adjustments and attitude changes a permanent part of your behavior. You'll become impervious to pressure situations and all but eliminate stress in your life. Repeat as directed. Why make yourself crazy?

400
Take stock.

Every once in a while, lay in bed a few extra minutes, or stop whatever you're doing, and take stock of where you are. Think of your accomplishments, the obstacles you've overcome, the mistakes you've corrected, the blessings you've been given. Be thankful for your good health and the loved ones in your life. This doesn't mean you should rest on your laurels, but at least give yourself some credit for how far you've come. So periodically take a mental inventory of everything good in your life...and don't let current troubles cloud your greater achievements. Why make yourself crazy?

Bonus: 401
Discipline rationally, not angrily.

Don't wait until you're furious before disciplining your kids. By then you'll be too worked up to apply any constructive punishment...and more likely to shout, hit and even abuse. Instead, reprimand bad behavior early on, before it, and your reaction to it, get out of hand. The kids can then learn from the discipline, and you'll save yourself untold aggravation and regret by remaining calm and in control. Why make yourself crazy?

Bonus: 402
Put time to work for you.

We always look at time as something working against us. There's never enough of it. It rushes in and pressures us. It becomes our enemy. But there's another side to time, whose passage we should welcome for the ills it cures. Time soothes bruised feelings, diminishes failure, scoffs at embarrassment, and conspires to fill the voids in our lives. It defuses the threat of anger and resentment, heals wounds physical and emotional, and lets in light where the outlook is dim. Take comfort in the knowledge that difficulties you now face will soon surrender to regenerative forces of time. Why make yourself crazy?

Bonus: 403
If it's broke, fix it.

Nothing gets more neglected than minor repairs. They can stare us in the face for years. But letting them wait robs you of more than full use of the item involved. Things like sighing toilets and wobbly garden gates eat away at your sense of order and serenity. Get into the habit of taking care of it right away. Just making an appointment with the repairperson will ease your mind (unless of course the guy doesn't show). Even more satisfying, fix it yourself. Upkeep is as good for the mind as it is for the home. Why make yourself crazy?

Bonus: 404
Be more forgiving of people.

Don't be poised to jump all over someone the minute they make a mistake or don't deliver exactly what you want. People can't read our minds. Nor do they always perform flawlessly. (Do you?) If someone is really trying, cut them a break. Save the eye-rolling, peevishness and complaints for when it's really justified, not just as a stock reaction to every minor glitch that befalls you. Be realistic and build the likelihood of human error into your expectations. Why make yourself crazy?

Bonus: 405
Have ample space for things.

Are your closets, drawers and cabinets so crammed that when you take things out you can never fit them back in again? When you acquire something new do you have absolutely no place to put it? This is an extremely frustrating way to live. You've got no room to maneuver. You constantly have to move things to get to other things. There's always something in the way, or falling out and clattering to the floor. You feel handcuffed, encumbered, oppressed. Look. The answer isn't getting more space. Because you can probably scrap half of this stuff and never miss it. Which would free up all sorts of room to allow you to live spaciously and efficiently. Don't let your possessions squeeze you out. It's not a warehouse. It's your home. Why make yourself crazy?

Bonus: 406
Don't be so self-conscious.

Most people aren't judging you. In fact, they're usually so wrapped up in the business at hand, or in their *own* image, they're barely noticing what you're wearing, how you're coming off, or that everything isn't just so. To prove it, think how easily you dismiss (or don't even notice) the minor flaws of others in light of their bigger, more positive traits. Being self-conscious needlessly distracts you from your larger purpose. Accept that your presentation will always have imperfections. They actually make you more human, more likable. Lighten up, be natural. Why make yourself crazy?

Bonus: 407
Don't pay before the
work is completed.

No matter whom you're hiring—painter, service technician, caterer, contractor—hold back the last installment until the work is finished to your satisfaction. That way you'll still have leverage if there's a problem. Take away the monetary incentive and you're inviting shoddy work, delays, loss of interest, and an unfinished job. No matter how nice and well-intentioned your vendor may seem, avoid paying it all up front. Why make yourself crazy?

Bonus: 408
Don't view life as cyclical.

It can make it seem dull, routine and predictable. And it's not. Instead, view your life as a straight line stretching off toward the future. What's to come has never happened before. Even holidays and traditions will be different because you can make them so. Prejudging the way things will play out only contributes to making them dull and uneventful. Or utterly disappointing. Surprise yourself. Shed your jaded notions and resist falling into the same tired thinking patterns that rob your life of vitality and diversity. Why make yourself crazy?

Bonus: 409
Please, get the amount
of sleep you need.

You can't cheat sleep. What you don't get in rest you'll pay for in diminished alertness, poorer performance, drowsiness, and irritability. And you'll have to make up your sleep debt anyway! Why fight this? Get into the habit of knocking off early (there are few things in life that can't wait till tomorrow), get a good night's sleep (usually about 7 to 8 hours, but no more since it is now known that *too much* sleep isn't good, either), and start the day rested, refreshed and ready to do your best. Why make yourself crazy?

Bonus: 410
Carve out time each
day for yourself.

"I have no time to myself" is a common refrain. Whose fault is that? First, you have to accept that personal time is a necessity, not a luxury, or you'll never leave yourself any. We all need some kind of break each day...to get away from work, chores, people, even family. Depriving yourself of "me time" will only leave you feeling ornery and resentful. Besides, how else can we properly evaluate what we're doing, see the big picture, appreciate those we love, unless we stand back from them once in a while? Take your allotted number of timeouts. Why make yourself crazy?

Bonus: 411
Stop worrying about your age.

Forget about the number of years you might be racking up. Your age has more to do with what you eat, how much you exercise and what your approach to life is than mere chronology. Worrying about it will only add to that feeling of agedness you're laying on yourself. Time is going to advance inexorably no matter what you do. Fortunately, you have power over how it will or won't affect you. Use that power. Why make yourself crazy?

Bonus: 412
Take responsibility for your own life.

It's easy to blame family members, coworkers, governments and everybody else when things don't go right for you. In fact, pointing the finger has become one of the more unattractive traits of our society. Don't hide behind a litany of excuses and accusations; instead, take responsibility for the choices and decisions you make. The sooner you do, the sooner you'll be able to recognize your mistakes, correct them and move on to better things. Why make yourself crazy?

Bonus: 413
Do what needs to be
done first...first.

This should be automatic, but for many reasons, we'll put off more important and pressing things to take care of lesser priorities first. Not only does it leave that bigger thing hanging over us, it often deprives us of the time and energy we'll need to accomplish the important task. Every morning, take a few moments to consider what project would make most sense to get out of the way first. Then meet it head on, without becoming sidetracked, without trying to squeeze something else in between. Then go on to the next most critical...and watch the stress ease away. Why make yourself crazy?

Bonus: 414
Make waiting worthwhile.

Cussing, fretting and agonizing never made waiting go any faster, and actually prolongs it. But using that downtime productively will. So when you're stuck in traffic, far back in line, or waiting for someone to show up...think of these moments as opportunities, not obstructions. Review and fine tune your plans for the day. Observe the world around you for its beauty, interest and ideas. Or just take a deep breath, relax and enjoy this unplanned time to yourself. In other words, turn what you normally might treat as a negative experience into a positive one. Why make yourself crazy?

Bonus: 415
Life is a bakery.

There are so many tempting things to taste, you wish you could try them all. If you did this at the bakery, of course, you'd soon be sick to your stomach. Yet in life we often exhibit no such restraint, grabbing and devouring everything in sight. The stress that ensues is the stomachache of our indulgence. And in our surfeited, half-crazed state, we barely enjoy what we're doing anyway, pinballing from one thing to the next, not even knowing exactly why. Life is sweet. Savor each of its offerings unhurriedly, in its own time, in its own way, in the manner it was meant to be enjoyed. Why rush? Like the baker's, there will always be something new to try, always plenty of treats in store. Why make yourself crazy?

Bonus: 416
More than ever, read the fine print.

Today, many companies—even some who were formerly reputable—are falling all over themselves trying to dupe us into accepting deals that are less than they're cracked up to be. Banks, car dealers, phone companies, retailers, service companies, and many other businesses—especially those on the Internet— deserve the closest of scrutiny. Trust no one. Watch out for surprise fees, hidden clauses, inflated claims, inadequate warranties, and shoddy support services. Read the fine print, ask the pointed questions, *before* you sign up. It's a lot less taxing than extricating yourself from a lousy deal, or getting retribution, later on. Why make yourself crazy?

* * * *

Save on Corporate, Group and Bulk Sales.

400 Ways to Stop Stress Now...and Forever! can be purchased direct from the publisher at quantity discounts.

The book makes an excellent educational and self-improvement guide for corporate stress management programs, health groups, schools, professional associations, government agencies, and many other types of groups and organizations.

The book also makes a valued giveaway at seminars and special events, or a premium for marketing promotions.

For more information, or to order, call **203-254-7789**, email **pickmeupbooks@aol.com** or visit:

www.pickmeupbooks.com

About the Author

G. Gaynor (Jerry) McTigue is the author of six books, including the best-selling *Life's Little Frustration Book* series (St. Martin's Press). His books have been featured on hundreds of radio and TV shows throughout the U.S. and Canada. Based on the same strategies presented in this book, McTigue conducts life-altering stress elimination workshops for groups and organizations. He has also written numerous articles and essays that have helped millions of people improve the quality and enjoyment of their lives. His work has appeared in major city newspapers and national magazines including *The Los Angeles Times, New York Daily News, Chicago Sun-Times, Philadelphia Inquirer, Miami Herald, Boston Globe, Travel-Holiday Magazine, Advertising Age,* and many others. He is a former columnist for America Online and a member of the American Society of Journalists and Authors (ASJA).

G. Gaynor McTigue is available for media interviews, book signings and speaking engagements. He can be reached at: jerrym321@aol.com

Also by G. Gaynor McTigue

Life's Little Frustration Book St. Martin's Press

You Know You're Middle Aged When... Pinnacle Books

More Life's Little Frustration Book St. Martin's Press

How Not To Make Love To A Woman Dove Books

Why Make Yourself Crazy? Pick Me Up Books

Printed in the United States
55811LVS00006B/109-153